FRENCH SHORT STORIES

30 French Short Stories for Beginners to Improve Your French Vocabulary

DYLANE MOREAU

ISBN: 978-1-998024-01-8

PREFACE

Welcome to "**French Short Stories**," a carefully curated collection of 30 French short stories with **translations, vocabulary**, and **comprehension questions**. This book has been thoughtfully designed to provide an engaging and effective way for English learners to enhance their language skills while exploring the captivating world of French literature.

With **30 stories** in total, this book provides you with enough learning material for the next **30 days** if you learn one story a day. Suitable for higher beginners, this book is tailored to those who already possess a basic knowledge of French grammar and sentence structures. Each story in the book includes **multiple choice and short answer questions** that are designed to test comprehension and retention of the material. Additionally, an audio download for each story, recorded by a native French speaker (me), is included to provide learners with an opportunity to practice their listening skills at a comfortable pace.

The book features both multiple choice and short answer questions for each story. The multiple choice questions are suitable for learners of all levels, while the short answer questions are designed to challenge those with a higher level of proficiency. This allows for a more personalized learning experience that caters to the needs of learners at different stages of their language journey.

The stories cover a range of topics inspired by daily life, from a day in Paris to family, health, and more. By reading these short stories, you will be able to improve your language proficiency and gain confidence in your French abilities.

Whether you are a beginner or an intermediate learner, this book is the perfect tool to help you improve your reading, listening, and speaking skills.

I hope that you find this book to be a valuable resource in your French learning journey and that it inspires you to continue exploring the rich world of French literature.

Thank you for choosing "French Short Stories," and happy reading! Bonne lecture!

Dylane

HOW TO USE THIS BOOK

If you're looking to enhance your reading comprehension skills and vocabulary, then this book is ideal for you. To maximize your learning experience, here are some helpful tips:

- **Take advantage of the notes pages throughout the book.** Keep track of the vocabulary you learned, the questions you got right and the ones you got wrong. Come back to your notes often to review them.
- **Pace Yourself:** Instead of reading all the stories in one sitting, try reading one story per day. This way, you can take your time and focus on understanding each story thoroughly.
- **Answer the Questions:** For each story, there are two types of questions: multiple-choice and short answer. If you're a beginner, start with the multiple-choice questions, and as you progress, challenge yourself with the short answer questions. You can answer with a single word, a group of words, or even a complete sentence.
- **Pay Attention to Vocabulary:** Each story contains bolded words that are important to understanding the text. Make sure to pay attention to these words and refer to the vocabulary list provided at the end of each story to learn their meaning.
- **Improve Your Listening Skills:** Take advantage of the free audio download and listen to each story while simultaneously reading the text. This technique will help you connect spoken and written French and may even improve your pronunciation.

By following these tips, you'll be well on your way to improving your French reading and listening skills after 30 days.

Haven fun learning!

How to Use the Vocabulary Lists?

Each vocabulary list contains the relevant words for the topic and is presented following the story. The words are highlighted in bold within the text for easy identification.
To optimize your learning experience, here are some important things to consider when using the vocabulary list:

- Whenever possible, all nouns are converted to their singular form so you can easily recognize their gender. Some nouns, such as profession, have masculine and feminine forms.
- All adjectives are presented in both masculine and feminine forms.
- Verbs are listed in their infinitive form to help you recognize their base form.
- Additionally, each vocabulary word is accompanied by its part of speech when possible, which is indicated in the legend below.

Legend:

adj - adjective - **adjectif**
adv - adverb - **adverbe**
n - noun - **nom** (when both genders are given)
nf - feminine noun - **nom féminin**
nm - masculine noun - **nom masculin**
prép - preposition - **préposition**
v - verb - **verbe**

How to Download the Audio?

To download the audio for the stories, visit **www.theperfectfrench.com/french-short-stories-audios1** or scan the **QR code** below. After entering your email, the audio download will be sent directly to your inbox.

CHAPTER 1

On va prendre un café

Aujourd'hui, je vais **prendre un café** avec **mon amie** Léa. On **s'est rencontrées** à **l'université** il y a dix ans. On **a passé** beaucoup de **temps ensemble**. On **habitait** même ensemble pendant notre **dernière année** d'université. Maintenant, on habite dans deux villes différentes mais on essaie de se voir **de temps en temps**, au moins **une fois par mois** ou **tous les deux mois**.

Cet après-midi, on est allées dans **un** petit **café** qui vient juste d'ouvrir dans la rue principale. On a eu de la chance car il n'y avait pas beaucoup de monde. On a choisi **une** petite **table** près de la fenêtre.

J'avais un peu faim quand je suis arrivée **au comptoir** donc j'ai commandé **un café** avec **un peu de lait** et **un morceau de tarte aux pommes**. Léa a commandé **un expresso** et **un pain au chocolat**. **La serveuse** nous a apporté nos cafés et **nos pâtisseries** après quelques minutes. Pendant qu'on buvait notre café, on a parlé de notre **vie quotidienne** et de notre **travail**. Je viens de **déménager** et Léa vient de commencer un **nouveau** travail donc on avait beaucoup de choses à se raconter aujourd'hui.

Après deux heures à discuter, on a décidé d'aller **se promener au parc** situé à côté du café. On s'est promenées pendant une heure avant de nous dire **au revoir**. Léa devait aller chercher **ses enfants** à **l'école** et moi je devais **rentrer** pour préparer **le dîner**.

On va se voir au même café le mois prochain.

We Are Going For Coffee

Today, I'm going to have coffee with my friend Léa. We met at university ten years ago and spent a lot of time together. We even lived together during our last year of university. Now, we live in different cities, but we try to see each other from time to time, at least once a month or every two months.

This afternoon, we went to a small coffee shop that had just opened on the main street. We were lucky because there weren't many people there. We chose a small table near the window.

When I got to the counter, I was a little hungry, so I ordered a coffee with a bit of milk and a piece of apple pie. Léa ordered an espresso and a "pain au chocolat." The waitress brought us our coffees and pastries after a few minutes. While drinking our coffee, we talked about our daily lives and work. I just moved, and Léa just started a new job, so we had a lot to catch up on.

After two hours of chatting, we decided to take a walk in the park next to the café. We walked for an hour before saying goodbye. Léa had to pick up her kids from school, and I had to go home to prepare dinner.

We're going to meet at the same coffee shop next month.

Vocabulary

Prendre un café - To have coffee

Un ami - Une amie n - A friend

Se rencontrer v - To meet

L'université nf - The university

Passer du temps ensemble - To spend time together

Habiter v - To live

La dernière année - The last year

De temps en temps prép - From time to time

Une fois par mois - Once a month

Tous les deux mois - Every two months

Un café nm - A coffee shop - A coffee

Une table nf - A table

Le comptoir nm - The counter

Un peu de lait - A little bit of milk

Un morceau nm - A piece

Une tarte aux pommes nf - Apple pie

Un expresso nm - An espresso

Un pain au chocolat nm - A "pain au chocolat" - A pastry

La serveuse nf - The waitress

Une pâtisserie nf - A pastry

La vie nf - Life

Quotidien - Quotidienne adj - Daily

Le travail nm - Work

Déménager v - To move

Nouveau - Nouvelle adj - New

Une chose nf - A thing

Se promener v - To take a walk

Le parc nm - The park

Au revoir - Goodbye

Les enfants nm - The children

L'école nf - The school

Rentrer v - To go back home

Le dîner nm - Dinner

Multiple Choice Questions

1. **Qu'est-ce qu'elle va faire aujourd'hui ?**

   What is she going to do today?

   a) **Prendre un café avec son amie Léa** - *Have coffee with her friend Léa*

   b) **Aller au travail** - *To go to work*

   c) **Aller faire du shopping** - *Go shopping*

2. **Où se situe le café dans lequel les deux amies sont allées ?**

   Where is the café where the two friends went located?

   a) **Dans un centre commercial** - *In a shopping center*

   b) **Dans la rue principale** - *On the main street*

   c) **Dans un parc** - *In a park*

3. **Qu'est-ce qu'elle commande au comptoir ?**

   What did she order at the counter?

   a) **Un café avec du lait et un pain au chocolat** -
   Coffee with milk and a pain au chocolat

   b) **Un thé et une tarte aux pommes** - *Tea and an apple pie*

   c) **Un café avec un peu de lait et un morceau de tarte aux pommes** -
   Coffee with a bit of milk and a piece of apple pie

4. **Quand est-ce qu'elles vont se revoir ?**

   When will they see each other again?

   a) **Jamais** - *Never*

   b) **L'année prochaine** - *Next year*

   c) **Le mois prochain** - *Next month*

5. **Qu'est-ce que Léa doit faire après ?**

   What does Léa have to do afterwards?

   a) **Léa doit aller chercher ses enfants à l'école** -
   Léa has to pick up her children from school

   b) **Léa doit aller chercher son mari au travail** -
   Léa has to pick up her husband from work

   c) **Léa a un rendez-vous important** - *Léa has an important appointment*

Short Answer Questions

1. **Avec qui est-ce qu'elle va prendre un café aujourd'hui ?**
   With whom is she going to have a coffee today?

   _____

   _____

2. **Où est-ce qu'elles se sont rencontrées pour la première fois ?**
   Where did they first meet?

   _____

   _____

3. **Est-ce qu'elles habitent encore ensemble ?**
   Do they still live together?

   _____

   _____

4. **Qu'est-ce que Léa a commandé au comptoir ?**
   What did Léa order at the counter?

   _____

   _____

5. **Où est-ce qu'elles sont allées après ?**
   Where did they go afterwards?

   _____

   _____

CHAPTER 2

Un repas de famille

Dans **ma famille**, on aime bien **se retrouver tous ensemble pour dîner**. On mange ensemble toutes les six semaines. On est en général **une dizaine de personnes**. Il y a **ma sœur** et moi, **mes parents**, **mes grands-parents**, **mon oncle**, **ma tante** et **leurs** deux **enfants**, **mes cousins**. Même si on **s'entend bien**, on a tous **des personnalités** différentes.

Ma mère est souvent **stressée** lors de ces **repas**, car elle veut que tout le monde passe un bon moment. **Mon père raconte** toujours les mêmes histoires qu'on a déjà entendues plusieurs fois. Mon oncle **se plaint** que les jeunes ne veulent pas travailler. Je pense que c'est parce qu'il ne trouve pas d'employés pour sa compagnie. Ma tante **boit** toujours **trop de vin**. Après quelques verres, elle veut danser dans le salon. Mes cousins **jouent** aux jeux vidéo. Ma sœur et moi, on préfère **rester** à table pour **discuter** avec tout le monde.

Mais il y a quelques mois, un des repas ne s'est pas terminé **comme d'habitude**. Ma tante dansait dans le salon, elle **a trébuché** et elle **s'est cassé la jambe**. Tout le monde a paniqué et ma mère a immédiatement **appelé** une ambulance. Mon oncle a suivi **l'ambulance** en voiture avec mes cousins.

Ma tante a mis plusieurs mois à **récupérer** de **sa blessure**. Elle boit toujours du vin, mais elle ne danse plus dans le salon. Maintenant, elle **est comme** mon père car elle raconte toujours les mêmes **histoires** à chaque repas.

〜〜〜〜〜

A Family Dinner

In my family, we like to get together for dinner. We eat together every six weeks. We are usually about ten people. There's my sister and me, my parents, my grandparents, my uncle, my aunt and their two children, my cousins. Even though we get along well, we all have different personalities.

My mother is often stressed during these meals because she wants everyone to have a good time. My father always tells the same stories we have heard several times. My uncle complains that young people don't want to work. I think it's because he can't find employees for his company. My aunt always drinks too much wine. After a few glasses, she wants to dance in the living room. My cousins play video games. My sister and I prefer to stay at the table to talk with everyone.

But a few months ago, one of the meals didn't end as usual. My aunt was dancing in the living room, she tripped and broke her leg. Everyone panicked and my mother immediately called an ambulance. My uncle followed the ambulance by car with my cousins.

It took my aunt several months to recover from her injury. She still drinks wine but no longer dances in the living room. Now she's like my father because she always tells the same stories at every meal.

Vocabulary

Une famille nf - A family

Se retrouver v - To get together

Tous ensemble - All together

Pour dîner - To have dinner

Une dizaine de personnes - About ten people

Ma sœur nf - My sister

Mes parents nm - My parents

Mes grands-parents nm - My grandparents

Mon oncle nm - My uncle

Ma tante nf - My aunt

Leurs enfants nm - Their children

Mes cousins nm - My cousins

Bien s'entendre v - To get along well

Une personnalité nf - A personality

Ma mère nf - My mother

Être stressé(e) v - To be stressed

Un repas nm - A meal

Mon père nm - My father

Raconter v - To tell (a story)

Se plaindre v - To complain

Boire v - To drink

Trop adv - Too much

Du vin nm - Wine

Jouer v - To play

Rester v - To stay

Discuter v - To discuss

Comme d'habitude adv - As usual

Trébucher v - To stumble

Se casser v - To break

Une jambe nf - A leg

Appeler v - To call

Une ambulance nf - An ambulance

Récupérer v - To recover

Une blessure nf - An injury

Être comme - To be like

Une histoire nf - A story

Multiple Choice Questions

1. **Qu'est-ce que la famille aime faire ensemble ?**
   What does the family like to do together?
   a) **Aller au cinéma -** *Go to the cinema*
   b) **Regarder la télévision -** *Watch TV*
   c) **Dîner ensemble -** *Have dinner together*
   d) **Faire du sport -** *Play sports*

2. **Combien de grands-parents viennent aux dîners ?**
   How many garndparents come to the dinners?
   a) **Un -** *One*
   b) **Deux -** *Two*
   c) **Trois -** *Three*
   d) **Quatre -** *Four*

3. **Comment est sa mère lors des repas de famille ?**
   How is her mother at family dinners?
   a) **Elle est heureuse -** *She is happy*
   b) **Elle est stressée -** *She is stressed*
   c) **Elle est en colère -** *She is angry*
   d) **Elle est fatiguée -** *She is tired*

4. **Qu'est-ce que fait son oncle lors des repas de famille ?**
   What does the uncle do during family dinners?
   a) **Il se plaint -** *He complains*
   b) **Il danse dans le salon -** *He dances in the living room*
   c) **Il boit trop de vin -** *He drinks too much wine*
   d) **Il joue aux jeux vidéo -** *He plays video games*

5. **Qu'est-ce que sa tante s'est cassée ?**
   What did her aunt break?
   a) **La main -** *The hand*
   b) **Le pied -** *The foot*
   c) **Le doigt -** *The finger*
   d) **La jambe -** *The leg*

Short Answer Questions

1. **Combien de personnes sont généralement présentes au dîner ?**
   How many people are usually at the dinner?

   _____

   _____

2. **Qui est stressé lors de ces dîners ?**
   Who gets stressed during these dinners?

   _____

   _____

3. **Qu'est-ce que son père fait pendant les dîners ?**
   What does her father do during the dinners?

   _____

   _____

4. **Qu'est-ce que ses cousins font pendant le dîner ?**
   What do her cousins do during dinner?

   _____

   _____

5. **Qui s'est cassé la jambe il y a quelques mois ?**
   Who broke their leg a few months ago?

   _____

   _____

CHAPTER 3

Je n'aime pas cuisiner

Je n'aime pas **cuisiner**. Pour moi, c'est **une tâche** ennuyeuse. Je préfère **manger au restaurant** ou prendre **des plats à emporter**. Je sais que certains adorent **passer des heures** à **préparer** des **plats** élaborés et délicieux. Mais pour moi, ça me stresse et j'ai l'impression de perdre mon temps.

Malheureusement, je sais que je ne peux pas manger **à l'extérieur tout le temps**. C'est **cher** et ce n'est pas très **sain**. Donc, je me suis mise à chercher des solutions pour rendre **la cuisine** un peu plus agréable pour moi.

J'ai commencé à chercher **des recettes simples** et **rapides** à préparer. J'ai trouvé quelques plats qui peuvent être préparés en quelques minutes seulement. D'après moi, ils sont tout aussi **délicieux** que des plats plus **difficiles** à préparer.

J'ai aussi commencé à inviter des amis à cuisiner avec moi. Ça rend la tâche plus amusante et ça me permet de passer du temps avec les gens que j'aime. Et puis, j'**ai investi** dans de bons **ustensiles** de cuisine. Ça peut sembler **bête**, mais avoir des **couteaux** qui **coupent** bien et des **casseroles de qualité** rend la cuisine beaucoup plus facile et agréable.

Aujourd'hui, je ne dirais pas que j'aime cuisiner, mais j'ai appris à trouver des moyens de rendre cette tâche un peu plus **supportable**. Et puis, quand j'arrive à préparer un plat délicieux, je **suis fière** de moi. J'**économise** aussi beaucoup d'**argent**. Ça en vaut la peine.

I Don't Like Cooking

I don't like to cook. For me, it's a boring task. I prefer eating at restaurants or getting takeout. I know some people love spending hours preparing elaborate and delicious dishes. But for me, it stresses me out and makes me feel like I'm wasting my time.

Unfortunately, I know I can't eat out all the time. It's expensive and not very healthy. So, I started looking for solutions to make cooking a little more enjoyable.

I began looking for simple and quick recipes to prepare. I found some dishes that can be prepared in just a few minutes. In my opinion, they are just as delicious as more difficult dishes to prepare.

I also started inviting friends to cook with me. It makes the task more fun and allows me to spend time with the people I love. And then, I invested in good cooking utensils. It may sound silly, but having sharp knives and quality pots and pans makes cooking much easier and more enjoyable.

Today, I wouldn't say I love cooking, but I've learned to find ways to make this task a little more bearable. And then, when I manage to prepare a delicious dish, I'm proud of myself. I also save a lot of money. It's worth it.

Vocabulary

Cuisiner v - To cook

Une tâche nf - A task

Manger au restaurant - To eat at a restaurant

Un plat à emporter nm - Takeout food

Passer des heures - To spend hours

Préparer v - To prepare

Un plat nm - A dish

À l'extérieur adv - Outside

Tout le temps adv - All the time

Cher - Chère adj - Expensive

Sain - Saine adj - Healthy

La cuisine nf - Cuisine

Une recette simple nf - A simple recipe

Rapide adj - Fast/Quick

Délicieux - Délicieuse adj - Delicious

Difficile adj - Difficult

Investir v - To invest

Un ustensile nm - A utensil

Bête adj - Silly

Un couteau nm - A knife

Couper v - To cut

Une casserole nf - A pot

De qualité adj - High quality

Supportable adj - Bearable

Être fier - fière - To be proud

Économiser v - To save

L'argent nm - Money

Multiple Choice Questions

1. **Est-ce qu'elle aime cuisiner ?**
   Does she like to cook?
   a) **Oui, elle adore cuisiner -** *Yes, she loves to cook*
   b) **Non, elle trouve que cuisiner est ennuyeux -** *No, she finds cooking boring*
   c) **Elle n'a jamais cuisiné -** *She has never cooked*

2. **Où est-ce qu'elle préfère manger ?**

   Where does she prefer to eat?

   a) **Chez ses parents -** *At her parents' house*

   b) **Au restaurant -** *At restaurants*

   c) **Chez ses amis -** *At her friends' place*

3. **Qui est-ce qu'elle invite à cuisiner avec elle ?**

   Who does she invite to cook with her?

   a) **Des amis -** *Friends*

   b) **Ses voisins -** *Neighbors*

   c) **Les membres d'un club de cuisine -** *Members of a cooking club*

4. **Comment est-ce qu'elle a rendu la cuisine plus agréable pour elle ?**

   How did she make cooking more enjoyable for herself?

   a) **En cherchant des recettes simples et rapides à préparer -**
      By finding simple and quick recipes to prepare

   b) **En invitant des amis à cuisiner avec elle -**
      By inviting friends to cook with her

   c) **En investissant dans de bons ustensiles de cuisine -**
      By investing in good cooking utensils

   d) **Toutes les réponses précédentes sont correctes -**
      All of the above answers are correct

5. **Qu'est-ce qu'elle a acheté pour rendre la cuisine plus agréable ?**

   What did she buy to make cooking more enjoyable?

   a) **Des planches à découper -** *Cutting boards*

   b) **Des livres de recettes -** *Recipe books*

   c) **Des couteaux et des casseroles -** *Knives and pots*

Short Answer Questions

1. **Qu'est-ce qu'elle n'aime pas faire ?**

   What does she not like to do?

   _____

   _____

2. **Pourquoi est-ce qu'elle ne peut pas manger à l'extérieur tout le temps ?**
   Why can't she eat out all the time?

   _____

   _____

3. **Est-ce qu'elle aime cuisiner des plats difficiles ?**
   Does she like to cook difficult dishes?

   _____

   _____

4. **Qu'est-ce qu'elle a acheté ?**
   What did she buy?

   _____

   _____

5. **Quand est-ce qu'elle est fière d'elle ?**
   When is she proud of herself?

   _____

   _____

Notes

CHAPTER 4

Une journée à Paris

Je viens d'**emménager** à Paris pour mes études. Aujourd'hui, c'est la première journée où j'ai le temps de **visiter** cette **ville magnifique**. Je veux voir tous **les endroits touristiques**. Je commence ma journée en prenant **le métro** pour aller à **la tour Eiffel**, **le monument** le plus **célèbre** de la ville. Je prends **l'ascenseur** pour admirer **la vue**. C'est magnifique !

Après avoir pris des photos et admiré la vue, je me dirige vers **le quartier** du Marais pour découvrir ses **rues pavées** et ses **vieux magasins**. Je m'arrête pour **déjeuner** dans un petit café et je commande **une quiche lorraine**, accompagnée d'**un verre de vin rouge**.

Ensuite, je me rends au **musée du Louvre** pour admirer **les œuvres d'art** les plus célèbres du monde. Je ne savais pas que **la Joconde** était aussi petite !

Après le musée, je me promène **le long de** la Seine et je profite de la vue sur **la cathédrale** Notre-Dame. Malheureusement, je ne peux pas la visiter car elle est en reconstruction depuis **l'incendie** de 2019.

Pour terminer ma journée, je m'arrête dans un petit **restaurant** pour manger **une fondue au fromage** avec des **pommes de terre** et du **pain**.

C'était une journée bien remplie et je suis ravie d'avoir pu découvrir quelques-unes des **merveilles** de Paris. Mon estomac est aussi bien rempli. Je ne savais pas que **les plats français** étaient aussi **lourds**. J'ai hâte de voir ce que les autres jours me réservent dans cette ville **magique**.

～～～～～

A Day in Paris

I just moved to Paris for my studies. Today is the first day I have had time to visit this beautiful city. I want to see all the tourist spots. I start my day by taking the metro to the Eiffel Tower, the city's most famous monument. I take the elevator to admire the view. It's magnificent!

After taking photos and admiring the view, I head to the Marais district to explore its cobblestone streets and old shops. I stop for lunch in a small café and order a quiche Lorraine, accompanied by a glass of red wine.

Next, I go to the Louvre Museum to admire the world's most famous works of art. I didn't know that the Mona Lisa was so small!

After the museum, I stroll along the Seine and enjoy the view of Notre Dame Cathedral. Unfortunately, I can't visit it because it's been under reconstruction since the 2019 fire.

To end my day, I stop at a small restaurant to eat cheese fondue with potatoes and bread.

It was a busy day, and I'm delighted to have discovered some of Paris's wonders. My stomach is also full. I didn't know French dishes were so heavy. I can't wait to see what the other days have in store for me in this magical city.

Vocabulary

Emménager v - To move in

Visiter v - To visit

La ville nf - The city

Magnifique adj - Beautiful

Un endroit nm - A place

Touristique adj - Touristic

Le métro nm - The metro/The subway

La tour Eiffel nf - The Eiffel Tower

Un monument nm - A monument

Célèbre adj - Famous

Un ascenseur nm - An elevator

La vue nf - The view

Le quartier nm - The neighborhood

Une rue pavée nf - A cobblestone street

Un vieux magasin nm - An old store

Le déjeuner nm - Lunch

Une quiche lorraine nf - A quiche Lorraine

Un verre de vin rouge nm - A glass of red wine

Le musée du Louvre nm - The Louvre Museum

Une œuvre d'art nf - A work of art

La Joconde nf - The Mona Lisa

Le long de prép - Along

La cathédrale nf - The cathedral

Un incendie nm - A fire

Un restaurant nm - A restaurant

Une fondue au fromage nf - Cheese fondue

Des pommes de terre nf - Potatoes

Du pain nm - Bread

Une merveille nf - A wonder

Un plat français nm - A French dish

Lourd - Lourde adj - Heavy

Magique adj - Magical

Multiple Choice Questions

1. **Pourquoi est-ce qu'elle a emménagé à Paris ?**

   Why did she move to Paris?

   a) **Pour chercher du travail -** *To look for work*

   b) **Elle ne sait pas pourquoi -** *She doesn't know why*

   c) **Pour ses études -** *For her studies*

2. **Qu'est-ce qu'elle veut faire aujourd'hui ?**

   What does she want to do today?

   a) **Visiter tous les endroits touristiques -** *Visit all the tourist spots*

   b) **Prendre des photos de la ville -** *Take photos of the city*

   c) **Trouver un endroit pour manger -** *Find a place to eat*

3. **Où est-ce qu'elle s'est rendue après avoir déjeuné ?**

   Where did she go after having lunch?

   a) **Au musée d'Orsay -** *Orsay Museum*

   b) **Au musée du Louvre -** *Louvre Museum*

   c) **À la cathédrale Notre-Dame** *- Notre-Dame Cathedral*

4. **Qu'est-ce qu'elle a mangé pour dîner ?**

   What did she eat for dinner?

   a) **Une salade de fruits avec du fromage -** *Fruit salad with cheese*

   b) **Une fondue au fromage avec des pommes de terre et du pain -** *Cheese fondue with potatoes and bread*

   c) **Une crêpe au chocolat -** *Chocolate crepe*

5. **Comment est-ce qu'elle décrit sa journée à Paris ?**

   How does she describe her day in Paris?

   a) **Ennuyeuse et fatigante -** *Boring and tiring*

   b) **Courte et peu intéressante -** *Short and uninteresting*

   c) **Remplie de découvertes merveilleuses -** *Filled with wonderful discoveries*

Short Answer Questions

1. **Quel moyen de transport est-ce qu'elle a pris pour aller à la tour Eiffel ?**
   What means of transport did she take to get to the Eiffel Tower?

   _____

   _____

2. **Qu'est-ce qu'elle a commandé pour déjeuner ?**
   What did she order for lunch?

   _____

   _____

3. **Pourquoi est-ce qu'elle ne peut pas visiter Notre-Dame ?**
   Why can't she visit Notre Dame?

   _____

   _____

4. **Comment est la Joconde d'après elle ?**
   How is the Mona Lisa, according to her?

   _____

   _____

5. **Comment est-ce qu'elle décrit les plats français qu'elle a mangés ?**
   How does she describe the French dishes she ate?

   _____

   _____

CHAPTER 5

Les amis d'enfance

Lucas, Jules et Emma sont **des amis d'enfance**. Ils **ont grandi** ensemble dans le même **quartier** et **partagent** beaucoup de **souvenirs**. Aujourd'hui, ils sont tous les trois **adultes** et ont tous des **vies** bien différentes, mais ils continuent à **se voir** régulièrement.

Un jour, Lucas a proposé **une idée folle** à ses amis : **partir en voyage** ensemble pendant un mois. Jules et Emma étaient d'abord **sceptiques**, car ils ont tous des **emplois à plein temps** et des **responsabilités** à assumer. Mais Lucas a réussi à les **convaincre** en leur disant que c'était l'occasion parfaite pour **se retrouver** et créer de nouveaux souvenirs ensemble.

Ils ont donc tous les trois demandé **un mois de congé** à leurs travails et ont commencé à **planifier leur voyage**. Ils ont décidé de partir en **Asie**, **un continent** qu'aucun d'entre eux n'a encore exploré. Ils ont réservé **des billets d'avion** et ont commencé à chercher **des hôtels** et **des activités**.

Leur voyage a commencé par **la découverte** de Tokyo, **la ville** la plus peuplée du monde. Ils sont restés une semaine là-bas. **Le décalage horaire** était un peu difficile. Ensuite, ils ont passé dix jours en **Chine**, sept jours en **Thaïlande**, avant de passer une semaine à Bali avant de rentrer. **Les plages** magnifiques de Bali étaient parfaites pour se reposer avant de recommencer le travail.

Ils sont maintenant rentrés **chez eux** avec moins d'**argent** dans leur **compte en banque** mais avec des souvenirs **inoubliables**. Ils veulent repartir l'année prochaine mais seulement pendant deux semaines.

Childhood Friends

Lucas, Jules, and Emma are childhood friends. They grew up together in the same neighborhood and share many memories. Today, they are all adults with very different lives, but they still see each other regularly.

One day, Lucas proposed a crazy idea to his friends: to go on a trip together for a month. Jules and Emma were initially skeptical because they all have full-time jobs and responsibilities to fulfill. But Lucas managed to convince them by saying that it was the perfect opportunity to reconnect and create new memories together.

So the three of them asked for a month off from their jobs and started planning their trip. They decided to go to Asia, a continent that none of them had explored yet. They booked plane tickets and started looking for hotels and activities.

Their trip began with the discovery of Tokyo, the most populated city in the world. They stayed there for a week. The jet lag was a bit difficult to adjust to. Then, they spent ten days in China, seven days in Thailand, before spending a week in Bali before returning home. Bali's beautiful beaches were perfect for relaxing before returning to work.

They have now returned home with less money in their bank accounts but with unforgettable memories. They want to go on another trip next year, but only for two weeks.

Vocabulary

Des amis d'enfance nm - Childhood friends

Grandir v - To grow up

Un quartier nm - A neighborhood

Partager v - To share

Un souvenir nm - A memory

Un adulte - Une adulte n - An adult

Une vie nf - A life

Se voir v - To see each other

Une idée folle nf - A crazy idea

Partir en voyage v - To go on a trip

Sceptique adj - Skeptical

Un emploi à plein temps nm -
A full-time job

Une responsabilité nf - A responsibility

Convaincre v - To convince

Se retrouver v - To meet up

Un mois de congé nm -
A month of vacation time

Planifier leur voyage - To plan their trip

L'Asie nf - Asia

Un continent nm - A continent

Un billet d'avion nm - An airplane ticket

Un hôtel nm - A hotel

Une activité nf - An activity

La découverte nf - The discovery

La ville nf - The city

Le décalage horaire nm - Jet lag

La Chine nf - China

La Thaïlande nf - Thailand

La plage nf - The beach

Chez eux - At their home

L'argent nm - Money

Un compte en banque nm - A bank account

Inoubliable adj - Unforgettable

Multiple Choice Questions

1. **Qui sont les personnages principaux de l'histoire ?**

   Who are the main characters of the story?

   a) **Lucas, Emma et Marc -** *Lucas, Emma, and Marc*

   b) **Lucas, Jules et Emma -** *Lucas, Jules, and Emma*

   c) **Lucie, Jules et Emma -** *Lucie, Jules, and Emma*

   d) **Léo, Julien et Emma -** *Léo, Julien, and Emma*

2. **Comment se connaissent Lucas, Jules et Emma ?**

   How do Lucas, Jules, and Emma know each other?

   a) **Ils sont cousins -** *They are cousins*

   b) **Ils sont collègues de travail -** *They are work colleagues*

   c) **Ils sont voisins -** *They are neighbors*

   d) **Ils sont amis d'enfance -** *They are childhood friends*

3. **Qu'est-ce que Lucas propose à ses amis ?**

   What does Lucas suggest to his friends?

   a) **D'acheter une maison ensemble -** *To buy a house together*

   b) **De partir en voyage ensemble -** *To go on a trip together*

   c) **De commencer un business ensemble -** *To start a business together*

   d) **De faire du bénévolat ensemble -** *To do volunteer work together*

4. **Où est-ce que les amis décident de voyager ?**

   Where do the friends decide to travel to?

   a) **En Europe -** *Europe*

   b) **En Amérique du Sud -** *South America*

   c) **En Asie -** *Asia*

   d) **En Afrique -** *Africa*

5. **Combien de temps est-ce qu'ils sont restés à Tokyo ?**

   How long did they stay in Tokyo?

   a) **Une semaine -** *One week*

   b) **Deux semaines -** *Two weeks*

   c) **Trois semaines -** *Three weeks*

   d) **Un mois -** *One month*

Short Answer Questions

1. **Comment s'appellent les trois amis d'enfance ?**
   What are the names of the three childhood friends?

   _____

   _____

2. **Est-ce qu'ils ont grandi dans le même quartier ?**
   Did they grow up in the same neighborhood?

   _____

   _____

3. **Où est-ce qu'ils ont décidé d'aller en voyage ?**
   Where did they decide to go on their trip?

   _____

   _____

4. **Combien de temps est-ce qu'ils sont restés à Bali ?**
   How long did they stay in Bali?

   _____

   _____

5. **Combien de temps va durer leur prochain voyage ?**
   How long will their next trip last?

   _____

   _____

CHAPTER 6

Les fruits

Les fruits sont des aliments sains, colorés et de toutes **les formes**. Ils sont faciles à manger et sont très bons pour notre corps. Les fruits nous donnent **des vitamines** et des nutriments qui nous aident à **rester en bonne santé**.

Il y a beaucoup de différents types de fruits, comme **les pommes**, **les bananes**, **les oranges**, **les fraises** et **les raisins**.

Certains fruits peuvent être mangés avec **la peau** comme la pomme, **la poire** et les raisins. La banane et l'orange doivent être **épluchées**. Manger **la pelure** d'une banane ou d'une orange n'est pas très bon. La pelure est là pour **protéger** l'intérieur du fruit.

Chaque fruit a **une saveur** différente et peut être mangé seul ou avec d'autres fruits. Quand on mélange plusieurs fruits ensemble, on appelle ça **une salade de fruits**.

Les fruits peuvent aussi être mangés **cuits**. Les pommes sont bonnes pour faire **des tartes** et **des compotes**. Les bananes sont délicieuses seules ou mélangées dans **des smoothies** et **des desserts**.

Les oranges sont **riches** en vitamine C et peuvent être **pressées** pour faire **du jus frais**.

Les fraises sont souvent utilisées dans les desserts comme les tartes, **les pâtisseries** et **les crèmes glacées**. Certaines personnes les mangent **nature** ou avec de **la crème fraîche**. Les raisins sont souvent mangés comme **collation** ou utilisés pour faire **du vin**.

Les fruits sont délicieux, nutritifs et faciles à manger. Il faut manger plusieurs **portions** de fruits **chaque jour** pour avoir toutes les vitamines dont on a besoin.

Fruits

Fruits are healthy, colorful, and come in all shapes. They are easy to eat and very good for our bodies. Fruits give us vitamins and nutrients that help us stay healthy.

There are many different types of fruits, such as apples, bananas, oranges, strawberries, and grapes.

Some fruits can be eaten with the skin, such as apples, pears, and grapes. Bananas and oranges need to be peeled. Eating the peel of a banana or an orange is not very good. The peel is there to protect the inside of the fruit.

Each fruit has a different flavor and can be eaten alone or with other fruits. When you mix several fruits together, it's called a fruit salad.

Fruits can also be eaten cooked. Apples are good for making pies and compotes. Bananas are delicious on their own or mixed in smoothies and desserts.

Oranges are rich in vitamin C and can be squeezed to make fresh juice.

Strawberries are often used in desserts such as pies, pastries, and ice creams. Some people eat them alone with whipped cream. Grapes are often eaten as a snack or used to make wine.

Fruits are delicious, nutritious, and easy to eat. We should eat several servings of fruits every day to get all the vitamins we need.

Vocabulary

Un fruit nm - A fruit

Une forme nf - A shape

Une vitamine nf - A vitamin

Rester en bonne santé - To stay healthy

Une pomme nf - An apple

Une banane nf - A banana

Une orange nf - An orange

Une fraise nf - A strawberry

Un raisin nm - A grape

La peau nf - The skin

Une poire nf - A pear

Éplucher v - To peel

La pelure nf - The peel

Protéger v - To protect

Une saveur nf - A flavor

Une salade de fruits nf - A fruit salad

Cuire v - To cook

Une tarte nf - A pie

Une compote nf - A compote

Un smoothie nm - A smoothie

Un dessert nm - A dessert

Riche adj - Rich

Presser v - To squeeze

Un jus frais nm - Fresh juice

Une pâtisserie nf - A pastry

Une crème glacée nf - Ice cream

Nature adj - Plain

La crème fraîche nf - Whipped cream

Une collation nf - A snack

Du vin nm - Some wine

Une portion nf - A portion

Chaque jour - Every day

Multiple Choice Questions

1. **Pourquoi est-ce que les fruits sont importants pour notre corps ?**
    Why are fruits important for our body?
    a) **Parce qu'ils sont colorés** - *Because they are colorful*
    b) **Parce qu'ils sont faciles à manger** - *Because they are easy to eat*
    c) **Parce qu'ils nous donnent des vitamines et des nutriments -**
        Because they give us vitamins and nutrients

2. **Quels fruits peuvent être mangés avec leur peau ?**
    Which fruits can be eaten with their skin?
    a) **La pomme, la poire et les raisins** - *Apple, pear, and grapes*
    b) **La banane, la pomme et la fraise** - *Banana, apple, and strawberry*
    c) **L'orange, la pomme et la banane** - *Orange, apple, and banana*

3. **Quel fruit peut être mangé en crème glacée dans le texte ?**
    Which fruit can be eaten as ice cream in the text?
    a) **La banane** - *Banana*
    b) **La poire** - *Pear*
    c) **Les fraises** - *Strawberries*

4. **Comment est-ce qu'on appelle un mélange de plusieurs fruits ensemble ?**
    What do you call a mixture of several fruits together?
    a) **Une salade de légumes** - *A salad of vegetables*
    b) **Une salade de fruits** - *A fruit salad*
    c) **Un smoothie aux fruits** - *A fruit smoothie*

5. **Comment est-ce qu'on peut consommer les raisins ?**
    How can grapes be consumed?
    a) **Comme collation ou pour faire du vin** - *As a snack or to make wine*
    b) **Dans une tarte aux pommes** - *In an apple pie*
    c) **Dans une soupe de fruits** - *In a fruit soup*

Short Answer Questions

1. **Quels sont les fruits mentionnés dans le texte ?**
    What fruits are mentioned in the text?

    _____

    _____

2. **Est-ce qu'on peut manger la peau de l'orange ?**
    Can you eat the orange peel?

    _____

    _____

3. **Quel est le but de la peau d'un fruit ?**
    What is the purpose of the peel of a fruit?

    _____

    _____

4. **Qu'est-ce qu'une salade de fruits ?**
    What is a fruit salad?

    _____

    _____

5. **Comment est-ce qu'on peut utiliser les pommes en cuisine ?**
    How can apples be used in cooking?

    _____

    _____

Notes

CHAPTER 7

Mon frère

Mon frère s'appelle Nelson. Il a dix-neuf ans, mais il va avoir vingt ans le 19 novembre. Il est à **l'université** depuis l'âge de dix-huit ans. Il **étudie** pour **devenir docteur**. Il est **courageux**, je ne sais pas si je pourrais étudier pendant autant d'années. Il est vraiment **passionné** par ses **études**. Il travaille dur. Il est considéré comme l'un des meilleurs élèves de sa classe.

Je ne le vois pas souvent car il étudie à l'université **loin de** la maison. Il rentre pour **les grandes vacances** en juin et en juillet, ainsi que pour **les vacances de Noël** en décembre. Il n'a pas le temps de rentrer **les week-ends** car il étudie beaucoup pour **réussir ses examens**.

L'été dernier, il a trouvé **un stage** de quelques semaines à **l'hôpital** de la ville. Mes parents étaient contents qu'il fasse son stage ici plutôt qu'à proximité de l'université.

On essaie de s'appeler au moins une fois par semaine pour **rester en contact**. On s'écrit aussi tous les jours. Parfois, c'est juste **une vidéo** amusante ou **une photo**. Si on a **un repas de famille** quand il n'est pas là, on fait toujours **un appel vidéo** pendant quelques minutes pour lui dire bonjour.

C'est étrange d'être à la maison sans lui car je n'ai pas d'autre frère. Je suis **seule** avec mes parents maintenant. Je **m'entends bien** avec **mes parents** donc ce n'est pas un problème, mais mon frère me manque parfois.

My Brother

My brother's name is Nelson. He is nineteen years old, but he will turn twenty on November 19th. He has been at university since he was eighteen. He is studying to become a doctor. He is brave, I don't know if I could study for that many years. He is really passionate about his studies. He works hard. He is considered one of the best students in his class.

I don't see him often because he studies at a university far from home. He comes home for the summer holidays in June and July and the Christmas holidays in December. He doesn't have time to come home on weekends because he studies hard to pass his exams.

Last summer, he found an internship for a few weeks at the hospital in town. My parents were happy he did his internship here instead of near the university.

We try to call each other at least once a week to stay in touch. We also write to each other every day. Sometimes, it's just a funny video or a photo. If we have a family meal when he's not there, we always make a video call to say hello to him for a few minutes.

It's strange to be at home without him because I don't have any other brothers. I am alone with my parents now. I get along well with my parents, so it's not a problem, but I miss my brother sometimes.

Vocabulary

Mon frère nm - My brother

L'université nf - The university

Étudier v - To study

Devenir v - To become

Docteur - Docteure n - Doctor

Courageux - Courageuse adj - Brave

Passionné - Passionnée adj - Passionate

Les études nf - Studies

Loin de adv - Far from

Les grandes vacances nf - Summer break

Les vacances de Noël nf - Christmas holidays

Un week-end nm - A weekend

Réussir ses examens - To pass exams

Un stage nm - An internship

Un hôpital nm - A hospital

Rester en contact - To stay in touch

Une vidéo nf - A video

Une photo nf - A photo

Un repas de famille nm - A family meal

Un appel vidéo nm - A video call

Seul - Seule adj - Alone

Bien s'entendre v - To get along well

Les parents nm - The parents

Multiple Choice Questions

1. **Depuis quel âge est-ce qu'il est à l'université ?**
   Since what age has he been at the university?
   a) **Depuis ses 16 ans -** *Since he was 16 years old*
   b) **Depuis ses 17 ans -** *Since he was 17 years old*
   c) **Depuis ses 18 ans -** *Since he was 18 years old*
   d) **Depuis ses 19 ans -** *Since he was 19 years old*

2. **Que veut-il devenir ?**

   What does he want to become?

   a) **Docteur** - *Doctor*

   b) **Ingénieur** - *Engineer*

   c) **Professeur** - *Teacher*

   d) **Avocat** - *Lawyer*

3. **Comment est-ce qu'il est considéré dans sa classe ?**

   How is he considered in his class?

   a) **Comme l'un des pires élèves** - *As one of the worst students*

   b) **Comme un élève moyen** - *As an average student*

   c) **Comme l'un des meilleurs élèves** - *As one of the best students*

   d) **Comme un mauvais élève** - *As a bad student*

4. **Où est-ce qu'il a effectué un stage l'été dernier ?**

   Where did he do an internship last summer?

   a) **À proximité de l'université** - *Near the university*

   b) **Dans un hôpital de la ville** - *At a hospital in the city*

   c) **Dans une entreprise de la ville** - *At a company in the city*

   d) **À l'étranger** - *Abroad*

5. **Pourquoi est-ce que son frère ne rentre pas souvent à la maison ?**

   Why doesn't his brother come home often?

   a) **Parce qu'il travaille dans une entreprise loin de la maison -**
   Because he works in a company far from home

   b) **Parce qu'il n'aime pas la maison** - *Because he doesn't like the house*

   c) **Parce qu'il étudie beaucoup pour réussir ses examens -**
   Because he studies a lot to pass his exams

   d) **Parce qu'il préfère rester avec ses amis** - *Because he prefers to stay with his friends*

Short Answer Questions

1. **Quel est le nom de son frère ?**

   What is the name of her brother?

   _____

   _____

2. **Quel âge a son frère ?**

   How old is her brother?

   _____

   _____

3. **Quand est son anniversaire ?**

   When is his birthday?

   _____

   _____

4. **Qu'est-ce que son frère étudie ?**

   What is her brother studying?

   _____

   _____

5. **Est-ce que son frère vit près de chez elle ?**

   Does her brother live near her?

   _____

   _____

CHAPTER 8

Le vin

Le vin est **une boisson alcoolisée** appréciée dans le monde entier. En France, le vin est **un art** et **une tradition**. Il existe différentes **variétés** de vin : **le vin blanc, le rosé** et **le vin rouge**.

Le vin blanc **est fabriqué** à partir de **raisins blancs** et a **une couleur jaune pâle**. C'est un vin **frais** et **léger** qui est parfait pour **les apéritifs** et **les plats** de **fruits de mer**.

Le rosé est fabriqué à partir de **raisins rouges,** mais il est laissé moins longtemps en contact avec la peau, ce qui lui donne une couleur rose. C'est un vin léger et **fruité**, qui est souvent servi avec **des salades** ou **des plats d'été**.

Le vin rouge est fabriqué à partir de raisins rouges et **est** souvent **vieilli en fût de chêne**. C'est un vin **corsé** qui accompagne parfaitement **les viandes rouges** et **les plats riches**.

L'étiquette de la bouteille donne des informations sur le type de vin.

Les visites de **vignobles** et de **caves à vin** sont également populaires. Elles offrent la possibilité de découvrir comment le vin est fait. **Les dégustations** de vins font souvent parties de ces **visites**. Cela permet aux visiteurs de **goûter** différents types de vins.

Le vin est une boisson qu'on peut apprécier **avec modération** et avec une alimentation équilibrée. Il y a des vins pour tous **les goûts**, pour toutes **les occasions**, et à tous **les prix**. Certaines bouteilles de vin **coûtent** plusieurs milliers d'euros.

Wine

Wine is an alcoholic beverage appreciated all over the world. In France, wine is an art and a tradition. There are different varieties of wine: white, rosé, and red.

White wine is made from white grapes and has a pale yellow color. It is a fresh, light wine perfect for aperitifs and seafood dishes.

Rosé wine is made from red grapes, but it is left in contact with the skin for less time, which gives it a pink color. It is a light, fruity wine often served with salads or summer dishes.

Red wine is made from red grapes and is often aged in oak barrels. It is a full-bodied wine that pairs perfectly with red meats and rich dishes. The bottle label provides information about the type of wine.

Visits to vineyards and wine cellars are also popular. They give the opportunity to discover how wine is made. Wine tastings are often part of these visits. This allows visitors to taste different types of wines.

Wine is a drink that can be enjoyed in moderation and with a balanced diet. There are wines for all tastes, for all occasions, and at all prices. Some wine bottles cost several thousand euros.

Vocabulary

Le vin nm - Wine

Une boisson alcoolisée nf - An alcoholic beverage

Un art nm - Art

Une tradition nf - A tradition

Une variété nf - A variety

Le vin blanc nm - White wine

Le rosé nm - Rosé wine

Le vin rouge nm - Red wine

Être fabriqué(e) v - To be made

Les raisins blancs nm - White grapes

Une couleur nf - A color

Jaune pâle adj - Pale yellow

Frais - Fraîche adj - Fresh

Léger - Légère adj - Light

Un apéritif nm - An aperitif

Des fruits de mer nm - Seafood

Des raisins rouges nm - Red grapes

Fruité - Fruitée adj - Fruity

Une salade nf - A salad

Un plat d'été nm - A summer dish

Être vieilli(e) v - To be aged

En fût de chêne - In oak barrels

Corsé - Corsée adj - Full-bodied

Une viande rouge nf - Red meat

Un plat riche nm - A rich dish

Une étiquette nf - A label

Un vignoble nm - A vineyard

Une cave à vin nf - A wine cellar

Une dégustation nf - A wine tasting

Une visite nf - A visit

Goûter v - To taste

Avec modération - In moderation

Le goût nm - The taste

Une occasion nf - An occasion

Un prix nm - A price

Coûter v - To cost

Multiple Choice Questions

1. **Quel est le vin fabriqué à partir de raisins blancs ?**

   What is the wine made from white grapes?

   a) **Le vin rouge -** *Red wine*

   b) **Le rosé -** *Rosé wine*

   c) **Le vin blanc -** *White wine*

   d) **Le champagne -** *Champagne*

2. **Comment est fabriqué le rosé ?**

   How is rosé wine made?

   a) **À partir de raisins blancs -** *From white grapes*

   b) **À partir de raisins rouges, mais en laissant la peau plus longtemps -** *From red grapes, but leaving the skin on longer*

   c) **À partir de raisins rouges, mais en laissant la peau moins longtemps -** *From red grapes, but leaving the skin on less*

   d) **À partir d'un mélange de raisins rouges et blancs -** *From a mix of red and white grapes*

3. **Quel est le vin parfait pour les apéritifs et les plats de fruits de mer ?**

   What is the perfect wine for aperitifs and seafood dishes?

   a) **Le vin rouge -** *Red wine*

   b) **Le rosé -** *Rosé wine*

   c) **Le vin blanc -** *White wine*

   d) **Le champagne -** *Champagne*

4. **Quel est le vin souvent servi avec des salades ou des plats d'été ?**

   What wine is often served with salads or summer dishes?

   a) **Le vin rouge -** *Red wine*

   b) **Le rosé -** *Rosé wine*

   c) **Le vin blanc -** *White wine*

   d) **Le champagne -** *Champagne*

5. **Qu'est-ce que les visites de vignobles et de caves à vin offrent ?**

   What do vineyard and wine cellar tours offer?

   a) **La possibilité de découvrir comment le vin est fait -** *The possibility of discovering how wine is made*

   b) **Des vins à plusieurs milliers d'euros -** *Wines worth several thousand euros*

   c) **Des plats de fruits de mer gratuits -** *Free seafood dishes*

   d) **Une bouteille de vin gratuite -** *A free bottle of wine*

Short Answer Questions

1. **Est-ce que le vin est une boisson alcoolisée ?**
    Is wine an alcoholic beverage?

    _____

    _____

2. **Quels sont les trois types de vin ?**
    What are the three types of wine?

    _____

    _____

3. **Avec quels plats est-ce qu'on peut boire du vin rouge ?**
    With which dishes can we drink red wine?

    _____

    _____

4. **Qu'est-ce que l'étiquette de la bouteille de vin donne comme informations ?**
    What information does the label on a bottle of wine provide?

    _____

    _____

5. **Combien peuvent coûter certaines bouteilles de vin ?**
    How much can some bottles of wine cost?

    _____

    _____

CHAPTER 9

Mon téléphone est déchargé

Je suis en train de **marcher** dans la rue. J'**utilise** mon téléphone pour **aller** à mon **rendez-vous**. Je n'arrive jamais à trouver **mon chemin** sans **mon téléphone**. Après dix minutes, je **me rends compte** que mon téléphone **est déchargé**. Je ne sais pas comment j'ai pu oublier de le **charger** avant de partir.

Je commence à avoir peur car j'**ai besoin de** mon téléphone pour arriver à **ma destination**. Je ne sais pas du tout où aller. En plus, j'ai besoin d'**appeler un taxi** pour rentrer chez moi plus tard. Je **me sens perdue** sans mon téléphone.

J'ai **mon chargeur** avec moi donc j'ai juste besoin de trouver **un endroit** pour le charger. Après quelques minutes de marche, je trouve un café. Juste au moment où mon téléphone **s'éteint**. Je demande **au serveur** s'il y a **une prise disponible** et si je peux charger mon téléphone. Il me dit que oui donc je **commande** un café et je **m'installe** le temps que mon téléphone charge un petit peu.

Mon téléphone **s'allume** tout seul après quelques minutes. Je le laisse charger pour que ça aille plus vite. Je prends **le journal** sur **le comptoir** et je lis quelques **articles**. Ce n'est pas si mal de ne pas utiliser son téléphone pendant une heure.

Finalement, mon téléphone est assez chargé et je peux **reprendre mon chemin**. Dans le futur, je dois **penser** à vérifier que mon téléphone est chargé avant de partir. Surtout quand je dois l'utiliser pour **me rendre quelque part**.

~~~~~~~~

My Phone Is Dead

I am walking down the street. I am using my phone to get to my appointment. I never seem to be able to find my way without my phone. After ten minutes, I realize that my phone is almost dead. I don't know how I could have forgotten to charge it before leaving.

I start to get scared because I need my phone to get to my destination. I have no idea where to go. Plus, I need to call a taxi to go back home later. I feel lost without my phone.

I have my charger with me so I just need to find a place to charge it. After a few minutes of walking, I find a café. Just as my phone shuts down. I ask the waiter if there is an available outlet and if I can charge my phone. He says yes so I order a coffee and sit down while my phone charges a little bit.

My phone turns on by itself after a few minutes. I leave it to charge so it goes faster. I pick up the newspaper on the counter and read a few articles. It's not so bad not using your phone for an hour.

Finally, my phone is charged enough and I can continue on my way. In the future, I need to remember to check that my phone is charged before leaving. Especially when I need to use it to get somewhere.

Vocabulary

Marcher v - To walk

Utiliser v - To use

Aller v - To go

Un rendez-vous nm - An appointment

Mon chemin nm - My way

Un téléphone nm - A phone

Se rendre compte v - To realize

Être déchargé v - To be dead

Charger v - To charge

Avoir besoin de v - To need

Une destination nf - A destination

Appeler v - To call

Un taxi nm - A taxi

Se sentir perdu(e) v - To feel lost

Un chargeur nm - A charger

Un endroit nm - A place

S'éteindre v - To turn off

Un serveur - Une serveuse n - A waiter/A waitress

Une prise disponible nf - An available outlet

Commander v - To order

S'installer v - To settle in/ To sit

S'allumer v - To turn on

Un journal nm - A newspaper

Un comptoir nm - A counter

Un article nm - An article

Reprendre son chemin - To continue on my way

Penser v - To think

Se rendre v - To go

Quelque part adv - Somewhere

Multiple Choice Questions

1. **Pourquoi est-ce qu'elle utilise son téléphone en marchant dans la rue ?**
   Why is she using her phone while walking on the street?
   a) **Pour écouter de la musique** - *To listen to music*
   b) **Pour aller à un rendez-vous** - *To go to an appointment*
   c) **Pour regarder des vidéos** - *To watch videos*
   d) **Pour faire des appels téléphoniques** - *To make phone calls*

2. **Qu'est-ce qu'elle doit trouver pour charger son téléphone ?**
   What does she need to find to charge her phone?
   a) **Trouver un endroit pour acheter un nouveau téléphone -**
      Find a place to buy a new phone
   b) **Demander à un ami de lui prêter un téléphone chargé -**
      Ask a friend to lend her a charged phone
   c) **Trouver une prise électrique -** *Find an electrical outlet*
   d) **Acheter un nouveau chargeur pour son téléphone -** *Buy a new charger for her phone*

3. **Où est-ce qu'elle peut finalement charger son téléphone ?**
   Where can she finally charge her phone?
   a) **Dans une boutique de vêtements -** *In a clothing store*
   b) **Dans un parc -** *In a park*
   c) **Dans un café -** *In a café*
   d) **Dans une station-service** - *In a gas station*

4. **Qu'est-ce qu'elle fait pendant que son téléphone charge ?**
   What does she do while her phone is charging?
   a) **Elle commande un café et lit le journal -** *She orders coffee and reads the newspaper*
   b) **Elle parle avec le serveur -** *She talks with the server*
   c) **Elle fait une sieste -** *She takes a nap*
   d) **Elle regarde des vidéos sur son téléphone -** *She watches videos on her phone*

5. **Qu'est-ce qu'elle décide de toujours faire dans le futur ?**
   What does she decide to always do in the future?
   a) **De ne plus jamais utiliser son téléphone -** *To never use her phone again*
   b) **De toujours charger son téléphone avant de partir -**
      To always charge her phone before leaving
   c) **De ne plus jamais se rendre à un rendez-vous** - *To never go to an appointment again*
   d) **D'acheter un nouveau téléphone -** *To buy a new phone*

Short Answer Questions

1. **Où est-ce qu'elle se trouve au début du texte ?**

   Where is she located at the beginning of the text?

   _____

   _____

2. **Pourquoi est-ce qu'elle a besoin de son téléphone plus tard ?**

   Why does she need her phone later?

   _____

   _____

3. **Est-ce qu'elle a son chargeur avec elle ?**

   Does she have her charger with her?

   _____

   _____

4. **Où est-ce qu'elle va pour charger son téléphone ?**

   Where does she go to charge her phone?

   _____

   _____

5. **Qu'est-ce qu'elle commande au café ?**

   What does she order at the café?

   _____

   _____

Notes

CHAPTER 10

Un voyage au ski

La famille Dupond est partie pour **leur voyage** au ski. Ils ont attendu cela pendant des semaines. Ils ont préparé **leurs valises** il y a quelques jours et ils ont vérifié deux fois qu'ils n'ont rien oublié. Ils ont mis **leurs skis, leurs bâtons** et **leurs chaussures** dans la voiture, ainsi que **des vêtements chauds, des collations** et **des boissons** pour **le trajet**.

Pierre, **le papa**, est **un bon skieur** et est content d'apprendre à skier à sa femme et à ses enfants. Il a acheté **des forfaits** de **remontées mécaniques** pour toute la famille. Il a aussi réservé **des cours de ski** pour les enfants.

Annie, **la maman**, est heureuse de **passer du temps** avec sa famille dans un endroit magnifique et de **se reposer** dans **un chalet** confortable après avoir skié. Elle a préparé une liste de choses à faire pour chaque jour et a pris **des jeux de société** pour les soirées en famille.

Les enfants, Lucie et Nola, sont impatients de voir **la neige** pour la première fois. Ils ont vu des vidéos de personnes qui skient et sont pressés d'essayer. Ils ont également emporté **leur luge** et ont demandé à leurs parents de les emmener faire de la luge.

Ils sont en voiture depuis quelques heures déjà. Ils sont presque arrivés à **la station de ski**. Ils ont tellement hâte de commencer **leur aventure** au ski. Ils seront de retour dans dix jours avec beaucoup **de souvenirs** et **de photos** de leur voyage au ski.

～～～～～

A Ski Trip

The Dupond family has left for their ski trip. They have been waiting weeks for this. They packed their suitcases a few days ago and checked twice to make sure they didn't forget anything. They put their skis, poles, and boots in the car as well as warm clothes, snacks, and drinks for the trip.

Pierre, the dad, is a good skier and is happy to teach his wife and kids how to ski. He bought lift tickets for the whole family. He also booked ski lessons for the children.

Annie, the mom, is happy to spend time with her family in a beautiful place and relax in a comfortable chalet after skiing. She prepared a list of things to do for each day and brought board games for family evenings.

The children, Lucie and Nola, are excited to see snow for the first time. They have watched videos of people skiing and can't wait to try it. They also brought their sled and asked their parents to take them sledding.

They have been on the road for a few hours already. They are almost at the ski resort. They can't wait to start their ski adventure. They will be back in ten days with lots of memories and photos of their ski trip.

Vocabulary

Un voyage nm - A trip

Une valise nf - A suitcase

Des skis nm - Skis

Des bâtons nm - Ski poles

Des chaussures nf - Shoes

Des vêtements chauds nm - Warm clothing

Une collation nf - A snack

Une boisson nf - A drink

Un trajet nm - A journey

Le papa nm - Dad

Un bon skieur nm - A good skier

Un forfait nm - A ski pass

Une remontée mécanique nf - A ski lift

Un cours de ski nm - A ski lesson

La maman nf - Mom

Passer du temps v - To spend time

Se reposer v - To rest

Un chalet nm - A chalet

Un jeu de société nm - A board game

La neige nf - Snow

Une luge nf - A sled

La station de ski nf - The ski resort

Une aventure nf - An adventure

Un souvenir nm - A souvenir

Une photo nf - A photo

Multiple Choice Questions

1. **Pourquoi est-ce que la famille Dupond est partie en voyage ?**
   Why did the Dupond family go on a trip?
   a) **Pour rendre visite à des amis** - *To visit friends*
   b) **Pour faire de la randonnée** - *To go hiking*
   c) **Pour se reposer à la plage** - *To relax at the beach*
   d) **Pour faire du ski** - *To go skiing*

2. **Combien de temps est-ce qu'ils ont attendu leur voyage au ski ?**

   How long did they wait for their ski trip?

   a) **Quelques jours** - *A few days*

   b) **Quelques semaines** - *A few weeks*

   c) **Quelques mois** - *A few months*

   d) **Quelques années** - *A few years*

3. **Que contient leur voiture pour leur voyage au ski ?**

   What is in their car for their ski trip?

   a) **Rien car ils vont louer les skis** - *Nothing because they will rent skis*

   b) **Des skis, des bâtons et des chaussures de ski** - *Skis, poles, and ski boots*

   c) **Des vêtements froids, des collations et des boissons** -
   Cold clothes, snacks, and drinks

   d) **Un karaoké** - *A karaoke machine*

4. **Qui a acheté les forfaits de remontées mécaniques pour toute la famille ?**

   Who bought the lift tickets for the whole family?

   a) **Pierre, le papa** - *Pierre, the dad*

   b) **Annie, la maman** - *Annie, the mom*

   c) **Lucie, la fille** - *Lucie, the daughter*

   d) **Nola, le fils** - *Nola, the son*

5. **Qu'est-ce que les enfants veulent essayer pour la première fois ?**

   What do the children want to try for the first time?

   a) **La luge** - *Sledding*

   b) **Le snowboard** - *Snowboarding*

   c) **Le patinage sur glace** - *Ice skating*

   d) **Le ski** - *Skiing*

Short Answer Questions

1. **Qui est un bon skieur dans la famille Dupond ?**

   Who is a good skier in the Dupond family?

   _____

   _____

2. **Qu'est ce qu'Annie a pris pour les soirées en famille ?**
   What did Annie bring for family evenings?

   _____

   _____

3. **Qu'est-ce que Lucie et Nola ont demandé à leurs parents de faire ?**
   What did Lucie and Nola ask their parents to do?

   _____

   _____

4. **Pendant combien de temps la famille Dupond sera en voyage au ski ?**
   How long will the Dupond family be on their ski trip?

   _____

   _____

5. **Qu'est-ce que Pierre, le père de famille, a acheté pour toute la famille ?**
   What did Pierre, the father of the family, buy for the whole family?

   _____

   _____

CHAPTER 11

La journée de Laura

Laura est **une personne** très **occupée**. Elle a toujours **un emploi du temps chargé** avec beaucoup de **rendez-vous**. Elle doit se dépêcher pour **être à l'heure** et ne pas **arriver en retard**. Elle doit également **être organisée** pour ne pas oublier ses rendez-vous importants.

Le matin, Laura se lève tôt pour **se préparer**. Elle prend **une douche**, **se brosse les dents** et **s'habille** pour la journée. Elle prépare également **un petit déjeuner** rapide avant de partir pour son premier rendez-vous.

Au cours de la journée, Laura rencontre **des clients**, discute avec **ses collègues** et travaille sur **des projets importants**. Elle doit également **prendre des notes** pendant **les réunions** et répondre à **ses emails**. Bien souvent, elle ne voit pas la journée passer.

Après le travail, Laura a souvent des engagements personnels, comme **des activités sportives** ou des rendez-vous avec **des amis**. Elle doit alors gérer son temps pour tout faire. Ce soir par exemple, elle va à **un cours de yoga** avec son ami Christian et après ils vont **manger une pizza**.

Le soir, avant de se coucher, Laura prend le temps de **se détendre** en lisant **un livre** ou en regardant **un film**. Pour mieux dormir, elle fait toujours **une liste** de ce qu'elle doit faire **le lendemain**.

Même si Laura est très occupée, elle prend le temps de **se reposer** et de se détendre pour **être en forme** le lendemain. Elle sait que c'est important pour **sa santé physique** et **sa santé mentale**.

~~~~~~~~~

Laura's Day

Laura is a very busy person. She always has a busy schedule with a lot of appointments. She has to hurry to be on time and not be late. She also has to be organized so as not to forget her important appointments.

In the morning, Laura gets up early to get ready. She takes a shower, brushes her teeth, and dresses for the day. She also prepares a quick breakfast before leaving for her first appointment.

During the day, Laura meets with clients, talks with her colleagues, and works on important projects. She also has to take notes during meetings and answer her emails. Often, she doesn't even see the day go by.

After work, Laura often has personal commitments, such as sports activities or appointments with friends. She has to manage her time to get everything done. Tonight, for example, she's going to a yoga class with her friend Christian and then they'll have pizza.

In the evening, before going to bed, Laura takes time to relax by reading a book or watching a movie. To sleep better, she always makes a list of what she needs to do the next day.

Even though Laura is very busy, she takes the time to rest and relax to be in good shape the next day. She knows that it's important for her physical and mental health.

Vocabulary

Une personne occupée - A busy person

Un emploi du temps nm - A schedule

Chargé - Chargée adj - Busy

Un rendez-vous nm - An appointment

Être à l'heure - To be on time

Arriver en retard - To arrive late

Être organisé(e) v - To be organized

Se préparer v - To get ready

Une douche nf - A shower

Se brosser les dents v -
To brush one's teeth

S'habiller v - To get dressed

Un petit déjeuner nm - A breakfast

Un client nm - A client

Un - Une collègue n - A colleague

Un projet important nm -
An important project

Prendre des notes - To take notes

Une réunion nf - A meeting

Un email nm - An email

Une activité sportive nf - A sports activity

Un ami - Une amie n - A friend

Un cours de yoga nm - A yoga class

Manger une pizza - To eat a pizza

Se détendre v - To relax

Un livre nm - A book

Un film nm - A movie

Une liste nf - A list

Le lendemain nm - The next day

Se reposer v - To rest

Être en forme - To be in shape

La santé physique nf - Physical health

La santé mentale nf - Mental health

Multiple Choice Questions

1. **Pourquoi est-ce que Laura se lève tôt le matin ?**

   Why does Laura wake up early in the morning?

   a) **Pour promener son chien -** *To walk her dog*

   b) **Pour se préparer pour la journée -** *To get ready for the day*

   c) **Pour faire du yoga -** *To do yoga*

2. **Comment est-ce que Laura se détend avant de se coucher ?**

   How does Laura relax before going to bed?

   a) **En regardant un film -** *By watching a movie*

   b) **En prenant une douche -** *By taking a shower*

   c) **En faisant de l'exercice -** *By exercising*

3. **Qu'est-ce que Laura fait avant de dormir pour mieux dormir ?**

   What does Laura do before sleeping to sleep better?

   a) **Elle se brosse les dents -** *She brushes her teeth*

   b) **Elle fait une liste de ce qu'elle doit faire le lendemain -**
   She makes a list of what she needs to do the next day

   c) **Elle prend une douche froide -** *She takes a cold shower*

4. **Qu'est-ce qu'elle va manger ce soir ?**

   What is she going to eat tonight?

   a) **Une pizza -** *A pizza*

   b) **Des pâtes -** *Pasta*

   c) **Des sushis -** *Sushi*

5. **Pourquoi est-ce que Laura prend le temps de se reposer et de se détendre ?**

   Why does Laura take the time to rest and relax?

   a) **Pour être en forme le lendemain -** *To be in shape the next day*

   b) **Pour perdre du poids -** *To lose weight*

   c) **Pour gagner plus d'argent -** *To earn more money*

Short Answer Questions

1. **Est-ce que Laura se lève tôt ou tard ?**
   Does Laura get up early or late?

   _____

   _____

2. **Est-ce que Laura prend une douche le matin ?**
   Does Laura take a shower in the morning?

   _____

   _____

3. **Est-ce que Laura lit un livre avant de se coucher ?**
   Does Laura read a book before bed?

   _____

   _____

4. **Pourquoi est-il important pour Laura de se reposer et se détendre ?**
   Why is it important for Laura to rest and relax?

   _____

   _____

5. **Où est-ce que Laura va ce soir ?**
   Where is Laura going that evening?

   _____

   _____

CHAPTER 12

Les cours de français

Je viens d'arriver en France pour travailler dans **une entreprise internationale** et je réalise que je ne **parle** pas bien **la langue**. Je crois qu'**il est temps** de prendre **des cours de français**.

Le premier jour de cours, j'ai rencontré **ma professeure**, madame Lydia. Elle m'a donné **un test** pour **évaluer mon niveau** de français. J'ai répondu **correctement** à la moitié des **questions**.

J'ai commencé les cours ce lundi. Les cours sont **difficiles**, mais **j'apprends** beaucoup de choses. Madame Lydia se concentre sur **la grammaire, le vocabulaire, les expressions** mais surtout sur **la prononciation**.

Nous sommes cinq **étudiants** dans cette **classe**. On a tous les mêmes **difficultés** à apprendre la langue, mais au moins on peut **s'aider** mutuellement.

Après quelques semaines, je commence à **me sentir plus à l'aise** en parlant français. Je commence à comprendre **les conversations** que j'entends dans la rue. C'est aussi plus facile de parler plus **naturellement** avec mes collègues **francophones**.

Je vais continuer à prendre des cours mais je pense prendre **des cours de conversation**. Je commence à **bien connaître** la grammaire et le vocabulaire. J'ai encore quelques **problèmes** avec la conjugaison mais ma professeure dit que cela deviendra plus facile **avec le temps**.

J'espère que les cours de conversation m'aideront à avoir plus de **facilité** à parler avec **des inconnus**. Les conversations au travail sont faciles car je connais bien mes collègues et on parle souvent de la même chose. Mais parler avec des inconnus, c'est **différent**.

French Classes

I have just arrived in France to work in an international company and I realize that I don't speak the language well. I think it's time to take French classes.

On the first day of class, I met my teacher, Mrs. Lydia. She gave me a test to assess my level of French. I answered half of the questions correctly.

I started classes this Monday. The classes are difficult, but I am learning a lot. Mrs. Lydia focuses on grammar, vocabulary, expressions, but especially on pronunciation.

There are five of us in this class. We all have the same difficulties in learning the language, but at least we can help each other.

After a few weeks, I am starting to feel more comfortable speaking French. I am starting to understand the conversations I hear on the street. It's also easier to speak more naturally with my Francophone colleagues.

I will continue to take classes but I think I will take conversation classes. I am starting to know the grammar and vocabulary well. I still have some problems with conjugation, but my teacher says that it will become easier with time.

I hope that the conversation classes will help me to be more at ease speaking with strangers. Conversations at work are easy because I know my colleagues well and we often talk about the same things. But speaking with strangers is different.

Vocabulary

Une entreprise internationale nf - An international company

Parler v - To speak

La langue nf - The language

Il est temps - It's time

Un cours de français nm - A French class

Un professeur - Une professeure n - A teacher

Un test nm - A test

Évaluer v - To evaluate

Un niveau nm - A level

Correctement adv - Correctly

Une question nf - A question

Difficile adj - Difficult

Apprendre v - To learn

La grammaire nf - Grammar

Le vocabulaire nm - Vocabulary

Les expressions nf - Expressions

La prononciation nf - Pronunciation

Un étudiant - Une étudiante n - A student

Une classe nf - A class

Une difficulté nf - A difficulty

S'aider v - To help each other

Se sentir plus à l'aise - To feel more comfortable

Une conversation nf - A conversation

Naturellement adv - Naturally

Francophone adj - French-speaking

Bien connaître - To know well

Un problème nm - A problem

Un cours de conversation nm - A conversation class

Avec le temps - With time

La facilité nf - Ease

Un inconnu - Une inconnue n - A stranger

Différent - Différente adj - Different

Multiple Choice Questions

1. **Pourquoi est-ce qu'elle a décidé de prendre des cours de français ?**
   Why did she decide to take French classes?
   a) **Parce qu'elle veut apprendre une nouvelle langue -**
      Because she wants to learn a new language
   b) **Parce qu'elle travaille dans une entreprise internationale en France et ne parle pas bien la langue -**
      Because she works in an international company in France and does not speak the language well
   c) **Parce qu'elle veut voyager en France -** *Because she wants to travel to France*

2. **Quand est-ce qu'elle a commencé les cours ?**
   When did she start her classes?
   a) **Ce lundi -** *This Monday*
   b) **Ce mercredi -** *This Wednesday*
   c) **Ce vendredi -** *This Friday*

3. **Est-ce qu'elle a bien répondu aux questions ?**
   Did she answer the questions correctly?
   a) **Non, elle a mal répondu à toutes les questions -**
      No, she answered all the questions incorrectly
   b) **Elle a répondu correctement à la moitié des questions -**
      She answered half of the questions correctly
   c) **Oui, elle a répondu correctement à toutes les questions -**
      Yes, she answered all the questions correctly

4. **Sur quoi est-ce que la professeure se concentre ?**
   What does the teacher focus on?
   a) **La grammaire -** *Grammar*
   b) **Le vocabulaire -** *Vocabulary*
   c) **Les deux -** *Both*

5. **Pourquoi est-ce qu'elle veut prendre des cours de conversation ?**
   Why does she want to take conversation classes?
   a) **Parce qu'elle veut avoir plus de facilités pour les conversations -**
      Because she wants to be more comfortable in conversations
   b) **Parce qu'elle a encore quelques problèmes avec la conjugaison -**
      Because she still has some problems with conjugation
   c) **Parce qu'elle veut apprendre plus de vocabulaire -**
      Because she wants to learn more vocabulary

Short Answer Questions

1. **Dans quel pays est-ce qu'elle travaille ?**
   What country does she work in?

   _____

   _____

2. **Quel est le nom de sa professeure ?**
   What is the name of her teacher?

   _____

   _____

3. **Qu'est-ce que sa professeure lui donne le premier jour de cours ?**
   What does her teacher give her on the first day of class?

   _____

   _____

4. **Combien d'étudiants est-ce qu'il y a dans la classe ?**
   How many students are there in the class?

   _____

   _____

5. **Quel type de cours est-ce qu'elle va prendre après quelques semaines ?**
   What type of class will she take after a few weeks?

   _____

   _____

Notes

CHAPTER 13

Je suis malade

Je n'ai pas été **malade** depuis trois ans. Depuis quelques jours, je me sens **faible** et **fatiguée**. Mon corps est **lourd** et mes mouvements sont **lents**. Je n'ai pas d'**énergie**. J'ai aussi de **la fièvre** et **la tête qui tourne**. Je ne suis pas dans mon assiette.

Je suis allée chez **le médecin** hier. Après m'avoir examiné, il a confirmé que j'ai **la grippe**. Il m'a prescrit **des médicaments** et m'a conseillé de me reposer autant que possible. Il m'a également recommandé de **boire** beaucoup d'eau pour **rester hydratée** et de manger sainement pour booster **mon système immunitaire**. Il a dit que je ne devrais pas retourner au travail cette semaine.

Je suis maintenant chez moi, **couchée** dans mon canapé. J'essaye de suivre **les conseils** du médecin. C'est difficile de ne rien faire, mais je sais que c'est important pour **guérir** plus rapidement. Dès que je me sentirai un peu mieux, je commencerai à lire le roman que je veux lire depuis des mois.

Mes amis ont pris **des nouvelles** de moi et m'ont envoyé des messages. J'ai de la chance de les avoir. J'aimerais les voir mais je ne peux pas **sortir de chez moi** pour le moment. Je ne veux pas leur donner la grippe.

D'après le docteur, je peux sortir dans trois jours. Je crois que j'**aurai besoin** de ces trois jours pour **me sentir mieux**. Je commence à avoir faim, donc je pense que je commence à **aller mieux**.

I Am Sick

I haven't been sick for three years. For the past few days, I've been feeling weak and tired. My body is heavy, and my movements are slow. I have no energy. I also have a fever and feel dizzy. I'm not feeling well.

I went to the doctor yesterday. After examining me, he confirmed that I have the flu. He prescribed medication for me and advised me to rest as much as possible. He also recommended that I drink plenty of water to stay hydrated and eat healthy to boost my immune system. He said that I shouldn't go back to work this week.

I'm now at home, lying on the couch. I'm trying to follow the doctor's advice. It's hard to do nothing, but I know it's important to recover quickly. As soon as I feel a little better, I'll start reading the novel that I've wanted to read for months.

My friends have been checking in on me and sending me messages. I'm lucky to have them. I would like to see them, but I can't leave my house at the moment. I don't want to give them the flu.

According to the doctor, I can go out in three days. I think I'll need those three days to feel better. I'm starting to get hungry, so I think I'm starting to feel better.

Vocabulary

Malade adj - Sick

Faible adj - Weak

Être fatigué(e) v - To be tired

Lourd - Lourde adj - Heavy

Lent - Lente adj - Slow

L'énergie nf - Energy

La fièvre nf - Fever

La tête qui tourne nf - Dizziness (The head spinning)

Le médecin nm - Doctor

La grippe nf - Flu

Un médicament nm - Medicine

Boire v - To drink

Rester hydraté(e) v - To stay hydrated

Le système immunitaire nm - Immune system

Être couché(e) v - To be lying down

Un conseil nm - Advice

Guérir v - To heal

Des nouvelles nf - News

Sortir de chez moi - To leave my house

Avoir besoin v - To need

Se sentir mieux v - To feel better

Aller mieux v - To get better

Multiple Choice Questions

1. **Quand est-ce qu'elle a été chez le médecin ?**
   When did she go to the doctor?
   a) **Ce matin** - *This morning*
   b) **Cet après-midi** - *This afternoon*
   c) **Hier** - *Yesterday*
   d) **Avant**-hier - *The day before yesterday*

2. **Comment est-ce qu'elle se sent depuis quelques jours ?**
   How has she been feeling for the past few days?
   a) **Faible et fatiguée** - *Weak and tired*
   b) **En bonne santé** - *Healthy*
   c) **Plein d'énergie** - *Full of energy*
   d) **De mauvaise humeur** - *In a bad mood*

3. **Qui est-ce qui lui envoie des messages ?**
   Who sends her messages?
   a) **Son docteur** - *Her doctor*
   b) **Ses collègues** - *Her colleagues*
   c) **Ses amis** - *Her friends*
   d) **Ses parents** - *Her parents*

4. **Qu'est-ce que le médecin recommande ?**
   What does the doctor recommend?
   a) **De boire beaucoup d'alcool** - *To drink a lot of alcohol*
   b) **De se reposer autant que possible** - *To rest as much as possible*
   c) **De manger du chocolat** - *To eat chocolate*
   d) **De retourner au travail cette semaine** - *To go back to work this week*

5. **Pourquoi est-ce qu'elle ne peut pas sortir de chez elle pour voir ses amis ?**
   Why can't she leave her home to see her friends?
   a) **Parce qu'elle n'a pas envie de les voir** - *Because she doesn't want to see them*
   b) **Parce qu'elle est trop fatiguée** - *Because she is too tired*
   c) **Parce qu'elle a peur de leur donner la grippe** -
      Because she is afraid of giving them the flu
   d) **Parce qu'elle n'aime pas sortir de chez elle** -
      Because she doesn't like leaving her home

Short Answer Questions

1. **Depuis quand est-ce qu'elle n'a pas été malade ?**
   When was the last time she was sick?

   _____

   _____

2. **Quels sont ses symptômes ?**

   What are her symptoms?

   _____

   _____

3. **Quand est-ce qu'elle est allée chez le médecin ?**

   When did she go to the doctor?

   _____

   _____

4. **Que lui a prescrit le médecin ?**

   What did the doctor prescribe for her?

   _____

   _____

5. **Où est-elle maintenant ?**

   Where is she now?

   _____

   _____

CHAPTER 14

Arthur

Arthur **a dix ans** et il n'aime pas beaucoup **l'école**. Il trouve **les cours** ennuyeux et il a toujours du mal à se concentrer. Les deux choses qu'il aime le plus dans la vie, c'est **jouer au football** et jouer avec **son chien** Tofu.

Tofu est un petit chien adorable. Les parents d'Arthur l'ont adopté **au refuge** il y a deux ans. Arthur aime passer son temps libre à jouer avec lui **au parc** près de chez lui. Tofu adore jouer à **la balle**. Il doit encore apprendre à rapporter la balle à Arthur.

Tous les mercredis et tous les samedis, Arthur a **entraînement** de football. Sa mère vient le chercher à l'école avec **ses chaussures à crampons, son maillot**, et **sa gourde. Le terrain** de football se trouve à quelques minutes en voiture. Sa mère regarde toujours l'entraînement. Quand il ne pleut pas, elle prend Tofu avec elle. Tofu veut toujours **courir** après **le ballon de football**.

Depuis le début de **la saison**, son **équipe** a gagné quatre **matchs** sur six. Arthur a marqué trois **buts** pendant ces six matchs. C'est bien mais il aurait aimé marquer plus de buts. Ils ont un match tous les dimanches matin.

Arthur sait déjà ce qu'il veut faire plus tard. Il espère pouvoir jouer au football **professionnellement**. Il veut gagner **la Coupe du monde**. Sa mère dit toujours que c'est possible mais qu'il doit réussir à l'école avant de devenir **footballeur**. Cela le **motive** à avoir **de bonnes notes** à l'école.

Arthur

Arthur is ten years old and he doesn't like school very much. He finds the classes boring and he always has difficulty concentrating. The two things he loves most in life are playing soccer and playing with his dog Tofu.

Tofu is an adorable little dog. Arthur's parents adopted him from the shelter two years ago. Arthur loves spending his free time playing with him in the park near his house. Tofu loves playing fetch. He still has to learn to bring the ball back to Arthur.

Every Wednesday and every Saturday, Arthur has soccer practice. His mother picks him up from school with his cleats, jersey, and water bottle. The soccer field is only a few minutes away by car. His mother always watches the practice. When it's not raining, she brings Tofu with her. Tofu always wants to chase the ball.

Since the beginning of the season, his team has won four out of six matches. Arthur has scored three goals during these six matches. It's good, but he would have liked to score more goals. They have a match every Sunday morning.

Arthur already knows what he wants to do in the future. He hopes to be able to play soccer professionally. He wants to win the World Cup. His mother always says it's possible but he has to succeed in school before becoming a soccer player. This motivates him to get good grades in school.

Vocabulary

Avoir ... ans - To be ... years old

L'école nf - School

Un cours nm - A class

Jouer au football - To play soccer

Un chien nm - A dog

Un refuge nm - A shelter

Un parc nm - A park

Une balle nf - A ball

Un entraînement nm - A practice/training session

Des chaussures à crampons nf - Cleats

Un maillot nm - A jersey/shirt

Une gourde nf - A water bottle

Le terrain nm - The field

Courir v - To run

Un ballon de football nm - A football/soccer ball

Une saison nf - A season

Une équipe nf - A team

Un match nm - A match/game

Un but nm - A goal

Professionnellement adv - Professionally

La Coupe du monde nf - The World Cup

Un footballeur nm - A soccer player

Motiver v - To motivate

Une bonne note nf - A good grade/mark

Multiple Choice Questions

1. Quelles sont les deux choses préférées d'Arthur ?

   What are Arthur's two favorite things?

   a) **Jouer aux jeux vidéo et regarder la télévision -** *Playing video games and watching TV*

   b) **Jouer au football et jouer avec son chien Tofu -** *Playing soccer and playing with his dog Tofu*

   c) **Lire des livres et écouter de la musique -** *Reading books and listening to music*

   d) **Faire du vélo et dessiner -** *Riding a bike and drawing*

2. Où est-ce que les parents d'Arthur ont adopté Tofu ?

   Where did Arthur's parents adopt Tofu?

   a) **Chez un éleveur de chiens -** *From a dog breeder*

   b) **Dans une animalerie -** *From a pet store*

   c) **Au refuge -** *From a shelter*

   d) **Dans la rue -** *From the street*

3. Où est-ce qu'Arthur joue avec Tofu ?

   Where does Arthur play with Tofu?

   a) **Dans la cour de l'école -** *In the school courtyard*

   b) **Au parc près de chez lui -** *In a park near his house*

   c) **À la bibliothèque -** *In the library*

   d) **Dans une salle de sport -** *In a gym*

4. Quand est-ce qu'Arthur a entraînement de football ?

   When does Arthur have soccer practice?

   a) **Tous les lundis et tous les jeudis -** *Every Monday and Thursday*

   b) **Tous les mardis et tous les vendredis -** *Every Tuesday and Friday*

   c) **Tous les mercredis et tous les samedis -** *Every Wednesday and Saturday*

   d) **Tous les jeudis et tous les dimanches -** *Every Thursday and Sunday*

5. Quel est le rêve d'Arthur pour l'avenir ?

   What is Arthur's dream for the future?

   a) **Devenir joueur de jeux vidéo professionnel -** *To become a professional video game player*

   b) **Devenir musicien -** *To become a musician*

   c) **Devenir acteur de cinéma -** *To become a movie actor*

   d) **Devenir footballeur professionnel et gagner la Coupe du monde -** *To become a professional soccer player and win the World Cup*

Short Answer Questions

1. **Quel âge a Arthur ?**
   What is Arthur's age?

   _____

   _____

2. **Est-ce qu'Arthur aime l'école ?**
   Does Arthur like school?

   _____

   _____

3. **Comment s'appelle le chien d'Arthur ?**
   What is the name of Arthur's dog?

   _____

   _____

4. **Combien de matchs est-ce que l'équipe d'Arthur a gagné ?**
   How many matches has Arthur's team won?

   _____

   _____

5. **Est-ce qu'Arthur sait ce qu'il veut faire plus tard ?**
   Does Arthur know what he wants to do in the future?

   _____

   _____

CHAPTER 15

On déménage

On **déménage** ! C'est une grande étape pour nous. On a trouvé un nouvel **appartement** dans **un quartier agréable** de la ville. Il est **plus grand** et **plus lumineux**. On a même **un petit jardin**.

On a commencé à préparer **le déménagement** il y a quelques semaines. On **a fait nos cartons**, **trié** les choses qu'on veut **garder** et celles qu'on veut **donner** ou **jeter**. C'était un peu fatigant mais c'était nécessaire. On avait beaucoup de choses dont on ne **se servait** pas.

Le jour du déménagement est arrivé. On **a loué un camion** pour transporter **nos affaires** et on a commencé à charger **les cartons**. Pour les choses lourdes et **les meubles**, on a utilisé **un diable**.

Une fois arrivés dans notre nouvel appartement, on a commencé à **décharger** le camion et à **ranger** nos affaires. On a seulement ouvert **les boîtes** dont on avait besoin directement comme **nos habits** et **les ustensiles de cuisine**. On **a** aussi **monté** le lit.

À la fin de la journée, on a mangé une pizza assis par terre car on n'a pas encore de table. Notre ancienne table était trop lourde. **Les locataires** de notre ancien appartement étaient contents de la garder.

On a passé les jours suivants à **explorer** notre nouveau quartier et à s'habituer à notre nouvel environnement. On a rencontré **des voisins** sympathiques et découvert des magasins et des restaurants intéressants.

On a encore une vingtaine de cartons à **déballer** et des meubles à **acheter** mais on se sent bien dans notre nouvel appartement.

~~~~~~

We Are Moving

We're moving! It's a big step for us. We found a new apartment in a nice neighborhood in the city. It's bigger and brighter. We even have a small garden.

We started preparing for the move a few weeks ago. We packed our boxes, sorted the things we want to keep and those we want to give away or throw away. It was a bit tiring but necessary. We had a lot of things we didn't use.

Moving day arrived. We rented a truck to transport our belongings and started loading the boxes. For heavy items and furniture, we used a dolly.

Once we arrived at our new apartment, we started unloading the truck and organizing our belongings. We only opened the boxes we needed right away like our clothes, kitchen utensils. We also assembled the bed.

At the end of the day, we ate pizza sitting on the floor since we don't have a table yet. Our old table was too heavy. The tenants in our old apartment were happy to keep it.

We spent the following days exploring our new neighborhood and getting used to our new environment. We met friendly neighbors and discovered interesting shops and restaurants.

We still have about twenty boxes to unpack and furniture to buy, but we feel good in our new apartment.

Vocabulary

Déménager v - To move

Un appartement nm - An apartment

Un quartier agréable nm -
A nice neighborhood

Plus grand - Bigger

Plus lumineux - Brighter

Un petit jardin nm - A small garden

Un déménagement nm - A move

Faire nos cartons - To pack our boxes

Trier v - To sort

Garder v - To keep

Donner v - To give

Jeter v - To throw away

Se servir v - To use

Louer v - To rent

Un camion nm - A truck

Des affaires nf - Belongings/Stuff

Un carton nm - A box

Des meubles nm - Furniture

Un diable nm - A trolley/A dolly

Décharger v - To unload

Ranger v - To arrange

Une boîte nf - A box

Des habits nm - Clothes

Des ustensiles de cuisine nm -
Kitchen utensils

Monter v - To assemble

Un locataire - Une locataire n - A tenant

Explorer v - To explore

Un voisin - Une voisine n - A neighbor

Déballer v - To unpack

Acheter v - To buy

Multiple Choice Questions

1. **Pourquoi est-ce qu'ils déménagent ?**

   Why are they moving?

   a) **Ils ont trouvé un nouvel emploi** - *They found a new job*

   b) **Ils n'aimaient pas leur ancien appartement** - *They didn't like their old apartment*

   c) **Ils ont trouvé un appartement plus grand et lumineux** - *They found a bigger and brighter apartment*

2. **Quel est l'avantage de leur nouvel appartement ?**

   What is the advantage of their new apartment?

   a) **Il a un petit jardin** - *It has a small garden*

   b) **Il est situé dans un quartier bruyant** - *It is located in a noisy area*

   c) **Il est plus petit que leur ancien appartement** - *It is smaller than their old apartment*

3. **Quand est-ce qu'ils ont commencé à préparer leur déménagement ?**

   When did they start preparing for their move?

   a) **Il y a quelques jours** - *A few days ago*

   b) **Il y a quelques semaines** - *A few weeks ago*

   c) **Il y a quelques mois** - *A few months ago*

4. **Comment ont-ils transporté les choses lourdes ?**

   How did they transport heavy items?

   a) **Ils ont tout porté à la main** - *They carried everything by hand*

   b) **Ils ont utilisé un diable** - *They used a dolly*

   c) **Ils ont engagé des déménageurs** - *They hired movers*

5. **Qu'est-ce qu'ils ont mangé le premier soir ?**

   What did they eat on the first night?

   a) **Une pizza** - *Pizza*

   b) **Rien** - *Nothing*

   c) **Des nouilles** - *Noodles*

Short Answer Questions

1. **Où se trouve le nouvel appartement ?**
   Where is the new apartment located?

   _____

   _____

2. **Comment est le nouvel appartement comparé au précédent ?**
   How does the new apartment compare to the previous one?

   _____

   _____

3. **Comment est-ce qu'ils ont transporté les meubles ?**
   How did they transport furniture?

   _____

   _____

4. **Quelles boîtes est-ce qu'ils ont ouvertes en premier ?**
   Which boxes did they open first?

   _____

   _____

5. **Pourquoi est-ce qu'ils ont mangé une pizza assis par terre ?**
   Why did they eat pizza sitting on the floor?

   _____

   _____

Notes

CHAPTER 16

Ma voiture est en panne

Hier, ma **voiture est tombée en panne**. J'étais en train de **conduire** sur **l'autoroute** quand j'ai entendu **un bruit étrange** qui venait de ma voiture. Tout à coup, la voiture a commencé à **ralentir** toute seule. J'ai mis **mes feux de détresse** et je **me suis garée** sur **le côté** de **la route**.

Je suis sortie de la voiture et j'**ai ouvert le capot** pour voir si je pouvais trouver quelque chose de bizarre. Malheureusement, je ne connais pas grand-chose en **mécanique** donc je n'ai pas trouvé **le problème**.

J'**étais coincée** sur le bord de la route. Je ne savais pas quoi faire. Mon téléphone n'avait plus **de batterie** donc je ne pouvais **appeler** personne. Je ne voyais pas non plus de **station-service** tout près.

J'étais en train de me demander comment j'allais faire pour sortir de cette **situation**, quand une voiture s'est arrêtée. C'était **un homme** sympathique qui m'a demandé si j'**avais besoin d'aide**.

Je lui ai expliqué mon problème et il m'a proposé de me **conduire** jusqu'à la station-service la plus **proche** pour appeler **un dépanneur**. J'étais soulagée et je l'ai remercié sincèrement.

Nous sommes arrivés à la station-service et j'ai réussi à **appeler** un dépanneur. Il lui a fallu quelques heures pour arriver donc j'ai pris **un café** et j'ai lu **un magazine**.

Finalement, le dépanneur est arrivé et il a réussi à **réparer** ma voiture. C'était un problème de batterie. J'étais soulagée de pouvoir enfin repartir sur **la route**.

Maintenant, je garde **un câble** pour **charger** mon téléphone dans la voiture.

～～～～～

My Car Broke Down

Yesterday, my car broke down. I was driving on the highway when I heard a strange noise coming from my car. Suddenly, the car started to slow down by itself. I turned on my hazard lights and parked on the side of the road.

I got out of the car and opened the hood to see if I could find anything suspicious. Unfortunately, I don't know much about mechanics so I couldn't find the problem.

I was stuck on the side of the road. I didn't know what to do. My phone was out of battery so I couldn't call anyone. I also didn't see a gas station nearby.

I was wondering how I was going to get out of this situation when a car stopped. It was a friendly man who asked me if I needed help.

I explained my problem to him, and he offered to drive me to the nearest gas station so that I could call a tow truck. I was relieved and thanked him sincerely.

We arrived at the gas station, and I managed to contact a tow truck. It took him a few hours to arrive so I had a coffee and read a magazine.

Finally, the tow truck arrived, and he managed to fix my car. It was a battery problem. I was relieved to be able to get back on the road finally.

Now, I keep a cable to charge my phone in my car.

Vocabulary

Une voiture nf - A car

Tomber en panne v - To break down

Conduire v - To drive

Une autoroute nf - A highway

Un bruit étrange nm - A strange noise

Des feux de détresse nm - Hazard lights

Se garer v - To park

Le côté nm - The side

La route nf - The road

Ouvrir v - To open

Le capot nm - The hood

La mécanique nf - Mechanics

Un problème nm - A problem

Être coincé(e) v - To be stuck

La batterie nf - The battery

Appeler v - To call

Une station-service nf - A gas station

Une situation nf - A situation

Un homme nm - A man

Avoir besoin d'aide v - To need help

Conduire v - To drive

Proche adj - Close

Un dépanneur nm - A tow truck

Appeler v - To call

Un café nm - A coffee

Un magazine nm - A magazine

Réparer v - To fix

La route nf - The road

Un câble nm - A cable

Charger v - To charge

Multiple Choice Questions

1. **Qu'est-ce qui est arrivé à la voiture ?**
   What happened to the car?
   a) **Elle est tombée en panne -** *It broke down*
   b) **Elle a eu un accident -** *It had an accident*
   c) **Elle est partie en fumée -** *It burst into flames*

2. **Qu'est-ce qu'il s'est passé quand la voiture a commencé à ralentir ?**
   What happened when the car started to slow down?
   a) **Elle a continué à rouler normalement -** *It continued to drive normally*
   b) **Elle s'est arrêtée toute seule -** *It stopped on its own*
   c) **Elle a accéléré brusquement -** *It suddenly accelerated*

3. **Comment est-ce qu'elle a réagi quand la voiture est tombée en panne ?**
   How did she react when the car broke down?
   a) **Elle a appelé un dépanneur tout de suite -**
      She called for a tow truck right away
   b) **Elle a ouvert le capot pour vérifier le moteur -**
      She opened the hood to check the engine
   c) **Elle a paniqué et ne savait pas quoi faire -**
      She panicked and didn't know what to do

4. **Pourquoi est-ce qu'elle n'a pas pu appeler quelqu'un avec son téléphone ?**
   Why couldn't she call anyone with her phone?
   a) **Parce qu'elle n'avait personne à appeler -** *Because she had no one to call*
   b) **Parce que son téléphone était cassé -** *Because her phone was broken*
   c) **Parce que son téléphone n'avait plus de batterie -**
      Because her phone ran out of battery

5. **Comment est-ce qu'elle a finalement réussi à appeler un dépanneur ?**
   How did she finally manage to call a tow truck?
   a) **En allant dans une station-service -** *By going to a gas station*
   b) **En demandant à l'homme qui l'a aidée de lui prêter son téléphone -**
      By asking the man who helped her to lend her his phone
   c) **En utilisant un téléphone public -** *By using a payphone*

Short Answer Questions

1. **Où est-ce qu'elle se trouvait quand sa voiture est tombée en panne ?**
   Where was she when her car broke down?

   _____

   _____

2. **Qu'est-ce qu'elle a entendu ?**
   What did she hear?

   _____

   _____

3. **Pourquoi est-ce qu'elle est allée à la station-service ?**
   Why did she go to the gas station?

   _____

   _____

4. **Qu'est-ce qu'elle a fait en attendant à la station-service ?**
   What did she do while waiting at the gas station?

   _____

   _____

5. **Quel était le problème de la voiture ?**
   What was the problem with the car?

   _____

   _____

CHAPTER 17

Être en bonne santé

Je me souviens de ma voisine, Camille. Elle aimait manger des bonbons et des frites, mais elle ne faisait pas beaucoup d'**exercice**. Elle **se sentait** souvent fatiguée et avait **des douleurs** dans les jambes.

Un jour, **son docteur** lui a dit qu'elle devait **prendre soin de sa santé**. Il lui a expliqué que pour **être en bonne santé**, il fallait manger **des aliments sains** et faire de l'**exercice** régulièrement. Camille a décidé d'écouter **les conseils** de son docteur et a commencé à changer **ses habitudes alimentaires**. Elle a commencé à manger plus **de fruits et légumes** et à éviter **les aliments gras** et **sucrés**.

Elle a également commencé à faire de l'exercice tous les jours. Elle **se promène** plus souvent, elle fait de **la danse** et des exercices de **musculation**. Elle a remarqué que plus elle faisait du sport, plus elle avait d'**énergie**.

Au fil du temps, Camille a commencé à **se sentir mieux**. Elle avait plus d'énergie et se sentait moins fatiguée. Elle n'avait plus de douleurs dans les jambes et se sentait en meilleure santé. Elle était **heureuse** d'avoir écouté les conseils de son docteur.

Maintenant, Camille continue à manger des aliments sains et à faire de l'exercice **régulièrement**. Elle se sent bien et elle est fière de prendre soin de **son corps**. Elle sait maintenant que la santé est la chose la plus importante dans la vie et qu'il est important de **prendre soin de soi**.

To Be in a Good Health

I remember my neighbor, Camille. She liked eating candy and fries but didn't exercise much. She often felt tired and had leg pains.

One day, her doctor told her she needed to care for her health. He explained that to be healthy, she needed to eat healthy foods and exercise regularly. Camille decided to listen to her doctor's advice and started to change her eating habits. She began to eat more fruits and vegetables and avoid fatty and sugary foods.

She also started exercising every day. She walks more often, dances, and does strength training. She noticed that the more she exercised, the more energy she had.

Over time, Camille began to feel better. She had more energy and felt less tired. She no longer had leg pains and felt healthier. She was happy to have listened to her doctor's advice.

Now, Camille continues to eat healthy foods and exercise regularly. She feels good and is proud to take care of her body. She now knows that health is the most important thing in life and that it is important to take care of oneself.

Vocabulary

De l'exercice nm - Exercise

Se sentir v - To feel

Une douleur nf **-** A pain

Un docteur nm - A doctor

Prendre soin de - To take care of

La santé nf - Health

Être en bonne santé -
To be in a good health

Des aliments sains nm - Healthy foods

Faire de l'exercice - To exercise

Un conseil nm **-** Advice

Des habitudes alimentaires nf **-**
Eating habits

Des fruits et légumes nm -
Fruits and vegetables

Les aliments gras nm - Fatty foods

Sucré - Sucrée adj - Sweet

Se promener v - To walk

La danse nf - Dance

La musculation nf - Weightlifting

L'énergie nf - Energy

Se sentir mieux v **-** To feel better

Heureux - Heureuse adj - Happy

Régulièrement adv - Regularly

Le corps nm - The body

Prendre soin de soi - Take care of yourself

Multiple Choice Questions

1. **Quelle était la nourriture préférée de Camille ?**
   What was Camille's favorite food?
   a) **Des fruits et légumes -** *Fruits and vegetables*
   b) **Des bonbons et des frites -** *Candies and fries*
   c) **Des gâteaux -** *Cakes*
   d) **Du poisson et du riz -** *Fish and rice*

2. **Pourquoi est-ce qu'elle se sentait souvent fatiguée ?**
   Why did she often feel tired?
   a) **Parce qu'elle faisait beaucoup d'exercice** - *Because she exercised a lot*
   b) **Parce qu'elle mangeait des aliments sains** - *Because she ate healthy foods*
   c) **Parce qu'elle ne faisait pas beaucoup d'exercice** -
      Because she didn't exercise much
   d) **Parce qu'elle dormait trop** - *Because she slept too much*

3. **Qui a conseillé à Camille de prendre soin de sa santé ?**
   Who advised Camille to take care of her health?
   a) **Son docteur** - *Her doctor*
   b) **Son voisin** - *Her neighbor*
   c) **Son professeur** - *Her teacher*
   d) **Son ami** - *Her friend*

4. **Que devait faire Camille pour être en bonne santé, selon son docteur ?**
   What did Camille need to do to be healthy, according to her doctor?
   a) **Manger des aliments gras et sucrés** - *Eat greasy and sweet foods*
   b) **Éviter les fruits et légumes** - *Avoid fruits and vegetables*
   c) **Faire de l'exercice régulièrement** - *Exercise regularly*
   d) **Regarder la télévision toute la journée** - *Watch TV all day*

5. **Comment est-ce que Camille se sent maintenant qu'elle prend soin de sa santé ?**
   How does Camille feel now that she's taking care of her health?
   a) **Elle se sent fatiguée et a des douleurs dans les jambes** -
      She feels tired and has leg pain
   b) **Elle se sent triste et déprimée** - *She feels sad and depressed*
   c) **Elle se sent frustrée** - *She feels frustrated*
   d) **Elle est heureuse et fière de prendre soin de son corps** -
      She is happy and proud to take care of her body

Short Answer Questions

1. **Qui est Camille ?**
   Who is Camille?

   _____

   _____

2. **Quels sont les aliments que Camille aimait manger ?**

   What are the foods that Camille liked to eat?

   _____

   _____

3. **Quels étaient les problèmes de santé de Camille ?**

   What were Camille's health problems?

   _____

   _____

4. **Qui a conseillé à Camille de prendre soin de sa santé ?**

   Who advised Camille to take care of her health?

   _____

   _____

5. **Quels sont les types d'exercices que Camille a commencé à faire ?**

   What types of exercises did Camille start doing?

   _____

   _____

CHAPTER 18

Acheter un cadeau

C'est **l'anniversaire** de mon ami Marc aujourd'hui et je veux lui **offrir un cadeau** utile et quelque chose qui lui **plaira**. J'ai beaucoup réfléchi à ce que je pourrais lui offrir et j'ai finalement décidé de lui **acheter un livre** dont il m'avait parlé.

La première **librairie** n'a pas le livre **en stock** mais la deuxième a **un exemplaire** seulement. Je l'achète et je rentre chez moi pour l'**emballer**. J'ai choisi un beau **papier cadeau** avec **un nœud**. Je lui écris **une petite note** pour lui **souhaiter un joyeux anniversaire**. J'ai aussi acheté **un bon d'achat** pour le petit café où il prend un café de temps en temps.

Le soir venu, je vais à **la fête d'anniversaire** de Marc. Il est ravi de me voir et nous passons une bonne **soirée** ensemble avec tous nos amis. Après avoir mangé **le gâteau**, c'est l'heure de **l'ouverture des cadeaux**.

Je lui tends **le paquet cadeau** et il l'**ouvre** impatiemment. Il est ravi de voir le livre qu'il voulait lire et il me remercie. Il me dit que c'est **parfait** car il voulait l'acheter demain.

C'est **chouette** de voir que Marc est **content** de son cadeau. J'aime offrir des cadeaux à mes amis, surtout quand le cadeau leur plaît. Je ne pense pas avoir offert un mauvais cadeau à quelqu'un mais **on ne sait jamais**. En général, on ne dit rien quand on n'aime pas un cadeau.

Quelques jours plus tard, Marc m'a envoyé **une photo** de son café accompagné de "**Merci** pour le café".

~~~~~~~~

Buying a Gift

It's my friend Marc's birthday today and I want to give him a useful gift and something he will like. I thought a lot about what I could give him and I finally decided to buy him a book he had talked to me about.

The first bookstore doesn't have the book in stock but the second one has only one copy. I buy it and go home to wrap it. I chose a beautiful wrapping paper with a bow. I write him a little note to wish him a happy birthday. I also bought a gift card for the small cafe where he has coffee from time to time.

In the evening, I go to Marc's birthday party. He is delighted to see me and we have a good evening together with all our friends. After eating the cake, it's time to open the gifts.

I hand him the gift package and he eagerly opens it. He is thrilled to see the book he wanted to read and thanks me. He says it's perfect because he was going to buy it tomorrow.

It's nice to see that Marc is happy with his gift. I like to give gifts to my friends, especially when the gift pleases them. I don't think I have ever given a bad gift to anyone, but you never know. Usually, people don't say anything when they don't like a gift.

A few days later, Marc sent me a photo of his coffee with the caption, "Thanks for the coffee."

Vocabulary

Un anniversaire nm - A birthday

Offrir v - To offer

Un cadeau nm - A gift

Plaire v - To please

Acheter v - To buy

Un livre nm - A book

Une librairie nf - A bookstore

En stock - In stock

Un exemplaire nm - A copy

Emballer v - To wrap

Du papier cadeau nm - Gift wrap

Un nœud nm - A bow

Une petite note nf - A little note

Souhaiter v - To wish

Un joyeux anniversaire nm - A happy birthday

Un bon d'achat nm - A gift card

Une fête d'anniversaire nf - A birthday party

Une soirée nf - An evening

Un gâteau nm - A cake

L'ouverture des cadeaux nf - The opening of gifts

Le paquet cadeau nm - The gift package

Ouvrir v - To open

Parfait - Parfaite adj - Perfect

Chouette adj - Cool/nice

Content - Contente adj - Happy/pleased

On ne sait jamais - You never know

Une photo nf - A photo

Merci - Thank you

Multiple Choice Questions

1. **Qui est Marc ?**

   Who is Marc?

   a) **Son ami -** *Her friend*

   b) **Un ami d'un ami -** *A friend of a friend*

   c) **Son petit copain -** *Her boyfriend*

2. **Pourquoi est-ce qu'elle a choisi ce cadeau pour Marc ?**

   Why did she choose this gift for Marc?

   a) **Parce qu'elle connaissait déjà le livre -**
   Because she already knew the book

   b) **Parce qu'elle était sûre que Marc voulait ce livre -**
   Because she was sure Marc wanted this book

   c) **Parce qu'elle voulait se débarrasser du livre -**
   Because she wanted to get rid of the book

3. **Pourquoi est-ce que la première librairie ne peut pas vendre le livre ?**

   Why can't the first bookstore sell the book?

   a) **Parce qu'elle est fermée -** *Because it's closed*

   b) **Parce qu'elle n'a pas de livres -** *Because it doesn't have books*

   c) **Parce qu'elle n'a pas ce livre en stock -** *Because it doesn't have the book in stock*

4. **Comment est-ce que Marc réagit à son cadeau ?**

   How does Marc react to his gift?

   a) **Il n'aime pas le cadeau -** *He doesn't like the gift*

   b) **Il est content -** *He is happy*

   c) **Il est surpris et confus -** *He is surprised and confused*

5. **Pourquoi est-ce que Marc la remercie quelques jours plus tard ?**

   What does Marc thank her for a few days later?

   a) **Pour le livre -** *For the book*

   b) **Pour le café -** *For the coffee*

   c) **Pour la soirée d'anniversaire -** *For the birthday party*

Short Answer Questions

1. **Quand est l'anniversaire de Marc ?**

   When is Marc's birthday?

   _____

   _____

2. **Qu'est-ce qu'elle a offert à Marc ?**

   What did she give Marc?

   _____

   _____

3. **Est-ce que la première librairie avait le livre en stock ?**

   Did the first bookstore have the book in stock?

   _____

   _____

4. **Est-ce qu'ils ont mangé un gâteau à la fête d'anniversaire ?**

   Did they eat cake at the birthday party?

   _____

   _____

5. **Qu'est-ce que Marc lui a envoyé quelques jours plus tard ?**

   What did Marc send to her a few days later?

   _____

   _____

Notes

CHAPTER 19

Une pizza

Une pizza, c'est **facile à faire**. Ce qui est bien avec les pizzas, c'est qu'on peut **ajouter** tous **les ingrédients** qu'on veut.

Pour faire une pizza, il faut **de la farine, de l'eau, de la levure, du sel** et **de l'huile d'olive**. Sur **la pâte**, on peut ajouter **de la sauce tomate, du fromage râpé, de la viande, des légumes** et **des herbes**.

Sophie adore les pizzas. Elle décide d'en faire une **pour dîner**. Elle n'**achète** jamais **de pizzas surgelées** car elle préfère les **faire maison**. Elle **mélange** la farine, la levure, le sel et l'eau pour faire **une pâte à pizza**. Elle ajoute de l'huile d'olive pour qu'elle soit **moelleuse**.

En attendant que la pâte **repose**, Sophie **prépare** la sauce tomate. Elle fait **chauffer** de l'huile d'olive, ajoute **de l'ail** et **des tomates pelées**, puis elle laisse **mijoter** la sauce pendant dix minutes.

Sophie **étale** la pâte sur **une plaque à pâtisserie** et la **couvre** de sauce tomate. Elle ajoute **des tranches** de **mozzarella, des champignons, des poivrons, des olives** et **du gruyère**. Elle voulait **ajouter** un peu d'**oignon** mais elle n'en a plus. Elle **saupoudre** un peu d'**origan** pour lui donner plus de **saveur**.

Sophie **met** la pizza **au four** et la laisse **cuire** pendant quinze minutes. Jusqu'à ce que **la croûte soit dorée** et **le fromage fondu**. Elle la sort du four et la laisse **refroidir** pendant quelques minutes. Elle **coupe** la pizza et s'installe devant la télé pour la manger.

～～～～～

A Pizza

A pizza is easy to make. What's great about pizzas is that you can add any ingredients you want.

To make a pizza, you need flour, water, yeast, salt, and olive oil. On the dough, you can add tomato sauce, grated cheese, meats, vegetables, and herbs.

Sophie loves pizzas. She decides to make one for dinner. She never buys frozen pizzas because she prefers to make them at home. She mixes flour, yeast, salt, and water to make the pizza dough. She adds olive oil to make it soft.

While waiting for the dough to rest, Sophie prepares the tomato sauce. She heats some olive oil, adds garlic and peeled tomatoes, and then lets the sauce simmer for ten minutes.

Sophie rolls out the dough onto a baking sheet and covers it with tomato sauce. She adds slices of mozzarella, mushrooms, bell peppers, olives, and gruyere cheese. She wanted to add some onion, but she ran out. She sprinkles a bit of oregano to give it more flavor.

Sophie puts the pizza in the oven and lets it cook for fifteen minutes until the crust is golden brown, and the cheese is melted. She takes it out of the oven and lets it cool for a few minutes. She cuts the pizza and settles in front of the TV to eat it.

Vocabulary

Facile à faire - Easy to make

Ajouter v - To add

Un ingrédient nm - An ingredient

De la farine nf - Flour

De l'eau nf - Water

De la levure nf - Yeast

Du sel nm - Salt

De l'huile d'olive nf - Olive oil

La pâte nf - Dough

De la sauce tomate nf - Tomato sauce

Du fromage râpé nm - Grated cheese

De la viande nf - Meat

Un légume nm - A vegetable

Une herbe nf - A herb

Pour dîner - For dinner

Acheter v - To buy

Une pizza surgelée nf - A frozen pizza

Faire maison - Homemade

Mélanger v - To mix

Une pâte à pizza nf - Pizza dough

Moelleux - Moelleuse adj - Soft

Reposer v - To rest

Préparer v - To prepare

Chauffer v - To heat up

De l'ail nm - Garlic

Une tomate pelée nf - Peeled tomato

Mijoter v - To simmer

Étaler v - To spread out

Une plaque à pâtisserie nf - Baking sheet

Couvrir v - To cover

Une tranche nf - A slice

De la mozzarella nf - Mozzarella

Un champignon nm - A mushroom

Un poivron nm - A bell pepper

Une olive nf - An olive

Du gruyère nm - Gruyere cheese

Un oignon nm - An onion

La croûte nf - The crust

Saupoudrer v - To sprinkle

Être doré(e) v - To be golden brown

De l'origan nm - Oregano

Le fromage fondu nm - Melted cheese

Une saveur nf - A flavor

Refroidir v - To cool down

Mettre au four v - To put in the oven

Couper v - To cut

Cuire v - To cook

Multiple Choice Questions

1. **Quels sont les ingrédients nécessaires pour faire une pizza ?**

   What are the necessary ingredients to make a pizza?

   a) **De la sauce tomate et du fromage -** *Tomato sauce and cheese*

   b) **Des légumes -** *Vegetables*

   c) **Tous les ingrédients qu'on aime -** *All the ingredients that we like*

2. **Quel est l'ingrédient principal de la sauce tomate de Sophie ?**

   What is the main ingredient in Sophie's tomato sauce?

   a) **Des tomates pelées -** *Peeled tomatoes*

   b) **De l'ail -** *Garlic*

   c) **De l'huile d'olive -** *Olive oil*

3. **Comment est-ce que Sophie fait cuire sa pizza ?**

   How does Sophie cook her pizza?

   a) **À la poêle -** *In a pan*

   b) **À la vapeur -** *Steamed*

   c) **Au four -** *In the oven*

4. **Quel ingrédient est-ce qu'il manque à Sophie pour sa pizza ?**

   What ingredient is missing for Sophie's pizza?

   a) **Du poivron -** *Bell pepper*

   b) **De l'oignon -** *Onion*

   c) **Des olives -** *Olives*

5. **Qu'est-ce que Sophie ajoute pour donner plus de saveur à sa pizza ?**

   What does Sophie do to add more flavor to her pizza?

   a) **Elle ajoute du basilic -** *She adds basil*

   b) **Elle ajoute de l'origan -** *She adds oregano*

   c) **Elle ajoute de la coriandre -** *She adds coriander*

Short Answer Questions

1. **De quoi est-ce qu'on a besoin pour faire une pâte à pizza ?**
   What do you need to make homemade pizza dough?

   _____

   _____

2. **Pourquoi est-ce que Sophie ne mange pas de pizzas surgelées ?**
   Why doesn't Sophie eat frozen pizzas?

   _____

   _____

3. **Qu'est-ce que Sophie ajoute pour que sa pâte soit moelleuse ?**
   What does Sophie add to make her dough soft?

   _____

   _____

4. **Quels ingrédients est-ce que Sophie ajoute à sa pizza ?**
   What ingredients does Sophie add to her pizza?

   _____

   _____

5. **Combien de temps est-ce que Sophie laisse mijoter la sauce tomate ?**
   How long does Sophie let the tomato sauce simmer?

   _____

   _____

CHAPTER 20

Une journée au parc

C'est une **belle** journée **ensoleillée** et les enfants **ont envie de** passer leur **journée** au parc. Leurs parents n'ont **rien de prévu** aujourd'hui donc ils acceptent. Ils commencent à préparer **des choses** à manger et à boire pour la journée.

Ils ont apporté des sandwichs, des fruits et des jus de fruits pour le pique-nique. Ils s'installent sur **une couverture** sous **un grand arbre** et commencent à manger. Les enfants jouent **tout près**. Ils s'amusent avec leur **nouveau cerf-volant**.

Après le pique-nique, les enfants veulent **jouer au football**. Ils se divisent en deux **équipes** : l'équipe des parents et l'équipe des enfants. Les parents **laissent** les enfants gagner 4-0.

Vers quatorze heures, ils vont faire **une promenade** dans le parc. Ils marchent le long **des sentiers**, en admirant **les arbres** et **les fleurs**. Ils s'arrêtent pour regarder **les canards** nager dans **l'étang** et **les tortues** qui attendent de recevoir à manger.

Après l'étang, ils arrivent à **l'aire de jeux**. Les enfants sont ravis. Cette aire de jeux a été installée il y a quelques mois. Elle est bien **mieux** que l'ancienne. Les enfants peuvent y passer des heures. Ils jouent sur **les balançoires**, **les toboggans** et **les échelles**.

Il est dix-sept heures. Il commence à être **tard**. Il est temps de rentrer. Ils ramassent leurs affaires et marchent tranquillement vers **la sortie** du parc. Les enfants sont fatigués et ils ont faim. Ils ont besoin d'un bain après avoir joué dans **l'herbe** pendant des heures. **La soirée** va être **courte** pour tout le monde.

~~~~~~~~

A Day at the Park

It's a beautiful sunny day, and the children want to spend their day at the park. Their parents have nothing planned for today, so they agree. They start preparing some food and drinks for the day.

They brought sandwiches, fruit, and fruit juices for the picnic. They settle on a blanket under a big tree and start eating. The children play nearby. They have fun with their new kite.

After the picnic, the children want to play soccer. They divide into two teams: the parents' team and the children's team. The parents let the children win 4-0.

Around two o'clock, they take a walk in the park. They walk along the paths, admiring the trees and flowers. They stop to watch the ducks swimming in the pond and the turtles waiting to be fed.

After the pond, they arrive at the playground. The children are thrilled. This playground was installed a few months ago. It's much better than the old one. The children can spend hours there. They play on swings, slides, and ladders.

It's 5 pm. It's starting to get late. It's time to go back. They gather their belongings and walk slowly toward the park's exit. The children are tired and hungry. They need a bath after playing in the grass for hours. The evening will be short for everyone.

Vocabulary

Beau - Belle adj - Beautiful

Ensoleillé - Ensoleillée adj - Sunny

Avoir envie de v - To want to

Une journée nf - A day

Rien de prévu - Nothing planned

Des choses nf - Things

Une couverture nf - A blanket

Un grand arbre nm - A big tree

Tout près adv - Very close

Nouveau - Nouvelle adj - New

Un cerf-volant nm - A kite

Jouer au football - To play soccer

Une équipe nf - A team

Laisser v - To let

Une promenade nf - A walk

Un sentier nm - A trail

Un arbre nm - A tree

Une fleur nf - A flower

Un canard nm - A duck

Un étang nm - A pond

Une tortue nf - A turtle

Une aire de jeux nf - A playground

Mieux adv - Better

Une balançoire nf - A swing

Un toboggan nm - A slide

Une échelle nf - A ladder

Tard adv - Late

La sortie nf - The exit

L'herbe nf - Grass

La soirée nf - The evening

Court - Courte adj - Short

Multiple Choice Questions

1. **Qu'est-ce que les parents ont préparé pour le pique-nique ?**
   What did the parents prepare for the picnic?
   a) **Des bonbons et des chips -** *Candies and chips*
   b) **Des sandwichs, des fruits et des jus de fruits -**
      Sandwiches, fruits, and fruit juices
   c) **Des pizzas et des boissons gazeuses -** *Pizzas and carbonated drinks*
   d) **Des hot-dogs et des sodas** *- Hot dogs and sodas*

2. **Avec quoi est-ce que les enfants jouent au parc ?**
   What are the children playing with at the park?
   a) **Un ballon -** *A ball*
   b) **Une tablette -** *A tablet*
   c) **Des cartes -** *Cards*
   d) **Un cerf-volant** *- A kite*

3. **Qu'est-ce qu'ils font après le pique-nique ?**
   What do they do after the picnic?
   a) **Ils jouent au football -** *They play soccer*
   b) **Ils font une promenade dans le parc -** *They take a walk in the park*
   c) **Ils regardent la télévision -** *They watch television*
   d) **Ils lisent des livres -** *They read books*

4. **Qu'est-ce que les enfants peuvent faire dans l'aire de jeux ?**
   What can the children do in the playground?
   a) **Regarder des films -** *Watch movies*
   b) **Faire du vélo -** *Ride a bike*
   c) **Jouer sur les balançoires, les toboggans et les échelles -**
      Play on swings, slides, and ladders
   d) **Jouer aux cartes -** *Play cards*

5. **Qui a gagné la partie de football ?**
   Who won the soccer game?
   a) **Les parents -** *The parents*
   b) **Les enfants -** *The children*

Short Answer Questions

1. **Qu'est-ce que les enfants veulent faire ?**
    What do the children want to do?

    _____

    _____

2. **Où est-ce qu'ils s'installent pour manger ?**
    Where do they settle to eat?

    _____

    _____

3. **Avec quoi est-ce que les enfants s'amusent après le pique-nique ?**
    What do the children have fun with after the picnic?

    _____

    _____

4. **Qu'est-ce qu'ils font après avoir joué au football ?**
    What do they do after playing soccer?

    _____

    _____

5. **Quels animaux est-ce qu'ils ont vu au parc ?**
    What animals did they see at the park?

    _____

    _____

CHAPTER 21

Au supermarché

Je suis allée **faire les courses** au **supermarché** ce matin. Les **placards** de la cuisine étaient **vides** donc je devais vraiment aller faire les courses. J'ai pris **mon caddie** et je suis entrée dans le **magasin**.

Je suis passée devant **le rayon** des **fruits et légumes**. Les couleurs vives et **l'odeur** des fraises ont attiré **mon attention**. J'ai acheté des fraises, des poires, des bananes, des carottes et des brocolis. Je suis sûre que ma famille appréciera un bon repas sain et équilibré.

Je suis ensuite allée dans **la section** des **produits laitiers**. J'ai acheté **du lait**, **des yaourts** et **du fromage**. J'aime beaucoup le fromage, donc j'ai pris **une variété de** fromages différents.

Ensuite, j'ai fait un tour dans **l'allée des pâtes**. Il y avait tellement **de choix** différents ! J'ai fini par prendre des pâtes au blé complet et de **la sauce tomate**.

J'ai terminé mes courses en passant par la section de **la boulangerie**. J'ai acheté **une baguette fraîche** pour accompagner le repas de ce soir.

Enfin, je me suis dirigée vers **les caisses** pour **payer mes achats**. **La caissière** était très gentille et m'a aidée à mettre mes courses dans **mes sacs**. J'apporte toujours mes propres sacs. Après avoir payé, la caissière m'a donné **mon ticket de caisse**. Je suis sortie du magasin avec mes sacs pleins et j'ai tout mis dans **le coffre** de ma voiture.

En rentrant chez moi, j'ai mis les courses dans **le frigo** et **le garde-manger** et j'ai commencé à préparer le dîner.

At the Supermarket

I went grocery shopping at the supermarket this morning. The kitchen cupboards were empty so I really had to go grocery shopping. I grabbed my cart and entered the store.

I walked past the fruit and vegetable aisles. The bright colors and the smell of strawberries caught my attention. I bought strawberries, pears, bananas, carrots, and broccoli. I'm sure my family will appreciate a good healthy and balanced meal.

Then, I went to the dairy section. I bought milk, yogurt, and cheese. I really like cheese, so I picked up a variety of different cheeses.

Next, I took a tour in the pasta aisle. There were so many different choices! I ended up picking whole wheat pasta and tomato sauce.

I finished my shopping by stopping by the bakery section. I bought a fresh baguette to go with tonight's dinner.

Finally, I went to the checkout to pay for my purchases. The cashier was very nice and helped me put my groceries in bags. I always bring my own bags. After paying, the cashier gave me my receipt. I walked out of the store with my full bags and put everything in the trunk of my car.

When I got home, I put the groceries in the fridge and pantry and started preparing dinner.

Vocabulary

Faire les courses - Grocery shopping

Un supermarché nm **-** A supermarket

Un placard nm **-** A cupboard

Vide adj **-** Empty

Un caddie nm **-** A shopping cart

Le magasin nm **-** The store

Un rayon nm **-** An aisle

Fruits et légumes - Fruits and vegetables

L'odeur nf **-** The smell

L'attention nf **-** Attention

Acheter v **-** To buy

La section nf **-** The section

Des produits laitiers nm **-** Dairy products

Du lait nm **-** Some milk

Des yaourts nm **-** Some yogurts

Du fromage nm **-** Some cheese

Une variété de nf **-** A variety of

Une allée nf **-** An aisle

Des pâtes nf **-** Some pasta

Un choix nm **-** A choice

De la sauce tomate nf **-** Tomato sauce

La boulangerie nf **-** The bakery

Une baguette fraîche nf **-** A fresh baguette

Les caisses nf **-** Checkout

Payer mes achats - To pay for my purchases

Le caissier - La caissière n **-** The cashier

Un sac nm **-** A bag

Un ticket de caisse nm **-** A receipt

Le coffre nm **-** The trunk

Le frigo nm **-** The fridge

Le garde-manger nm **-** The pantry

Multiple Choice Questions

1. **Qu'est-ce qu'elle a acheté au rayon des fruits et légumes ?**
   What did she buy in the fruits and vegetables section?
   a) **Des pommes de terre et des tomates -** *Potatoes and tomatoes*
   b) **Des fraises, des poires, des bananes, des carottes et des brocolis -** *Strawberries, pears, bananas, carrots and broccoli*
   c) **Des oranges et des kiwis -** *Oranges and kiwis*

2. **Qu'est-ce qu'elle a acheté dans l'allée des pâtes ?**
   What did she buy in the pasta aisle?
   a) **Des pâtes au blé complet et de la sauce tomate -** *Whole wheat pasta and tomato sauce*
   b) **Des pâtes et des boulettes de viande -** *Pasta and meatballs*
   c) **Des pâtes à la carbonara et du parmesan -** *Carbonara pasta and Parmesan cheese*

3. **Qu'est-ce qu'elle a pris pour accompagner le repas de ce soir ?**
   What did she take to accompany tonight's meal?
   a) **Un pain de mie -** *Sliced bread*
   b) **Une baguette fraîche -** *Fresh baguette*
   c) **Un croissant -** *Croissant*

4. **Pourquoi est-ce que la caissière l'a aidée à mettre ses courses dans ses sacs ?**
   Why did the cashier help her put her groceries in her bags?
   a) **Parce que la caissière était gentille -** *Because the cashier was kind*
   b) **Parce qu'il y avait du monde -** *Because there were many people*
   c) **Parce que la cliente avait mal au dos -** *Because the customer had a sore back*

5. **Où est-ce qu'elle a rangé ses courses en rentrant chez elle ?**
   Where did she store her groceries when she got home?
   a) **Dans le frigo et le garde-manger -** *In the fridge and pantry*
   b) **Dans le placard de la cuisine -** *In the kitchen cabinet*
   c) **Sur la table de la salle à manger -** *On the dining table*

Short Answer Questions

1. **Pourquoi est-ce qu'elle devait faire les courses ?**
    Why did she have to go grocery shopping?

    _____

    _____

2. **Quels fruits et légumes est-ce qu'elle a achetés ?**
    What fruits and vegetables did she buy?

    _____

    _____

3. **Qu'est-ce qu'elle a acheté dans la section des produits laitiers ?**
    What did she buy in the dairy section?

    _____

    _____

4. **Qu'est-ce qu'elle a acheté à la boulangerie ?**
    What did she buy at the bakery?

    _____

    _____

5. **Qu'est-ce qu'elle fait après avoir mis les courses dans le frigo et le garde-manger ?**
    What does she do after putting the groceries in the fridge and pantry?

    _____

    _____

Notes

CHAPTER 22

Il fait trop chaud

Il **fait** trop **chaud** en ce moment. C'est **la canicule**. **Les températures** atteignent presque **40 degrés**. **La chaleur** est **accablante**. On ne peut pas sortir **dehors**. Tout le monde cherche **des moyens** pour **se rafraîchir**. Il faut aussi boire beaucoup **d'eau** pour **rester hydraté**.

Je suis à la maison avec ma famille. On a décidé de passer la journée **à l'intérieur** pour **se protéger** de la chaleur. On a fermé **les rideaux** pour garder la maison **fraîche**. Tous **les ventilateurs** sont allumés pour faire circuler **l'air**.

Notre chien, Max, est allongé sur le sol. Il cherche aussi un peu de **fraîcheur**. C'est difficile pour **les animaux** de se rafraîchir quand il fait si chaud.

Beaucoup de mes amis sont à **la piscine**, comme beaucoup d'autres. J'ai vu les photos qu'ils ont postées sur internet. La piscine est **bondée**. Il y a une trentaine d'enfants dans l'eau. La piscine municipale n'est pas très grande donc elle est vite remplie.

Aux alentours de vingt heures, les températures commencent enfin à **baisser**. On sort de chez nous pour **profiter** de **la soirée**. On va manger dehors. On reste sur **notre terrasse** jusqu'à ce que le soleil **se couche**.

La canicule est **difficile**, mais tout le monde trouve des moyens de **s'adapter** et de rester au frais. La canicule devrait être finie la semaine prochaine d'après **la météo**. On espère avoir quelques jours de **pluie** car les forêts et les jardins **ont besoin d'eau**.

~~~~~~~~~

It's Too Hot

It's too hot right now. It's a heat wave. Temperatures are almost reaching 40 degrees. The heat is overwhelming. We can't go outside. Everyone is looking for ways to cool down. It's also important to drink a lot of water to stay hydrated.

I'm at home with my family. We decided to spend the day indoors to protect ourselves from the heat. We closed the curtains to keep the house cool. All the fans are on to circulate the air.

Our dog, Max, is lying on the floor. He's also looking for some coolness. It's difficult for animals to cool down when it's so hot.

Many of my friends are at the pool, as are many others. I saw the photos they posted on the internet. The pool is crowded. There are about thirty children in the water. The public pool is not very big so it fills up quickly.

Around eight o'clock, temperatures finally start to drop. We go out of our house to enjoy the evening. We'll eat outside and stay on our terrace until the sun sets.

The heat wave is difficult, but everyone finds ways to adapt and stay cool. According to the weather forecast, the heat wave should be over next week. We hope to have a few days of rain because the forests and gardens need water.

Vocabulary

Faire chaud v - To be hot

La canicule nf - Heatwave

La température nf - Temperature

Un degré nm - A degree

La chaleur nf - Heat

Accablant - Accablante adj - Overwhelming

Dehors adv - Outside

Un moyen nm - A way

Se rafraîchir v - To cool down

L'eau nf - Water

Rester hydraté(e) v - To stay hydrated

À l'intérieur prép - Inside

Se protéger v - To protect oneself

Un rideau nm - A curtain

Frais - Fraîche adj - Cool

Un ventilateur nm - A fan

L'air nf - Air

La fraîcheur nf - Coolness

Un animal - Des animaux nm - Animal/Animals

La piscine nf - Pool

Bondé(e) adj - Crowded

Baisser v - To decrease

Profiter v - To enjoy

La soirée nf - Evening

Une terrasse nf - A terrace

Se coucher v - To set

Difficile adj - Difficult

S'adapter v - To adapt

La météo nf - Weather forecast

La pluie nf - Rain

Avoir besoin d'eau - To need water

Multiple Choice Questions

1. **Quelle est la situation météorologique actuelle ?**

   What is the current weather situation?

   a) **Un ouragan -** *A hurricane*

   b) **Une tempête de neige -** *A snowstorm*

   c) **Une canicule -** *A heatwave*

   d) **Un orage -** *A thunderstorm*

2. **Que fait sa famille pour se protéger de la chaleur ?**

   What does the family do to protect themselves from the heat?

   a) **Ils vont à la piscine -** *They go to the pool*

   b) **Ils ferment les rideaux -** *They close the curtains*

   c) **Ils font du jogging -** *They go jogging*

   d) **Ils restent au lit -** *They stay in bed*

3. **Comment est-ce que Max, le chien, réagit à la chaleur ?**

   How does Max the dog react to the heat?

   a) **Il cherche un peu de fraîcheur -** *He seeks a little bit of coolness*

   b) **Il aime jouer sous le soleil -** *He likes to play under the sun*

   c) **Il n'est pas affecté par la chaleur -** *He is not affected by the heat*

   d) **Il préfère sortir se promener -** *He prefers to go out for a walk*

4. **Où est-ce que ses amis passent la journée pour se rafraîchir ?**

   Where do her friends spend the day to cool off?

   a) **À la bibliothèque -** *At the library*

   b) **À la plage -** *At the beach*

   c) **À la piscine municipale -** *At the public pool*

   d) **Au parc -** *At the park*

5. **Qu'est-ce qu'elle espère à la fin de la canicule ?**

   What does she hope for at the end of the heatwave?

   a) **De la neige -** *Snow*

   b) **Plus de soleil -** *More sun*

   c) **Un orage -** *A thunderstorm*

   d) **De la pluie -** *Rain*

Short Answer Questions

1. **Quelle est la température actuelle ?**
   What is the current temperature?

   _____

   _____

2. **Comment est la chaleur ?**
   How is the heat?

   _____

   _____

3. **Pourquoi est-ce qu'ils ont fermé les rideaux ?**
   Why did they close the curtains?

   _____

   _____

4. **Comment est la piscine ?**
   How is the pool?

   _____

   _____

5. **D'après la météo, quand est-ce que la canicule va être finie ?**
   According to the weather forecast, when will the heat wave be over?

   _____

   _____

CHAPTER 23

Un voyage dans le temps

Mia découvre **une vieille horloge** dans **le grenier** de **sa grand-mère**. Elle la **nettoie** et remarque qu'elle peut tourner **les aiguilles**. Elle décide de **tourner** les aiguilles **à l'envers** pour voir **ce qu'il se passe**.

Soudainement, elle **se retrouve** transportée **dans le temps**, elle est maintenant en 1820. Elle est surprise de voir **des costumes anciens et des voitures à chevaux**. Tout est **différent**. Elle rencontre une dame qui lui explique où elle se trouve. Mia n'arrive pas à y croire. La dame l'invite à prendre une tasse de thé.

Après quelques heures en 1820, Mia décide qu'il est temps de **rentrer** chez elle. Elle tourne les aiguilles de l'horloge dans **la bonne direction**. Soudainement, elle **est de retour** dans le grenier de sa grand-mère. Elle **est soulagée** d'être rentrée **chez elle**.

La nuit suivante, Mia décide de nouveau d'utiliser l'horloge pour **voyager** dans le temps. Cette fois-ci, elle tourne les aiguilles dans **l'autre sens** et se retrouve **transportée** dans les années 2160. Quelle **époque** incroyable ! Elle rencontre des gens qui lui expliquent comment **la technologie** a évolué. Ils lui montrent **des appareils incroyables**, tels que **des voitures volantes** et **des ordinateurs portables** ultra-compacts.

Après plusieurs jours à découvrir **les merveilles du futur**, il est temps de rentrer chez elle. Elle tourne les aiguilles dans la bonne direction et arrive dans le grenier. Peut-être que demain elle retournera dans **le futur**.

~~~~~~

A Journey Through Time

Mia discovers an old clock in her grandmother's attic. She cleans it and notices that she can turn the hands. She decides to turn the hands backwards to see what happens.

Suddenly, she finds herself transported in time and she is now in 1820. She is surprised to see old suits and horse-drawn carriages. Everything is different. She meets a lady who explains where she is. Mia can't believe it. The lady invites her for a cup of tea.

After a few hours in 1820, Mia decides it's time to go home. She turns the clock hands in the right direction and finds herself back in her grandmother's attic. She is relieved to be back home.

The next night, Mia decides to use the clock again to travel through time. This time, she turns the hands in the other direction and finds herself transported to the year 2160. What an incredible era! She meets people who explain to her how technology has evolved. They show her amazing devices such as flying cars and ultra-compact laptops.

After several days discovering the wonders of the future, it's time to go back home. She turns the hands in the right direction and arrives in the attic. Maybe tomorrow she will go back to the future.

Vocabulary

Une vieille horloge nf - An old clock

Le grenier nm - The attic

Une grand-mère nf - A grandmother

Nettoyer v - To clean

Une aiguille nf - A hand (of a clock)

Tourner v - To turn

À l'envers - Backwards

Ce qu'il se passe - What happens

Se retrouver v - To find oneself

Dans le temps - In time

Un costume ancien nm - An old suit

Une voiture à chevaux nf -
A horse-drawn carriage

Différent - Différente adj - Different

Rentrer v - To return

La bonne direction nf - The right direction

Être de retour - To be back

Être soulagé(e) v - To be relieved

Chez elle - At her home

La nuit nf - The night

Voyager v - To travel

L'autre sens nm - The other way

Être transporté(e) v - To be transported

Une époque nf - An era

Un appareil incroyable nm -
An incredible device

Une voiture volante nf - A flying car

Un ordinateur portable nm - A laptop

Une merveille du futur nf -
A wonder of the future

Le futur nm - The future

Multiple Choice Questions

1. **Qu'est-ce que Mia découvre dans le grenier de sa grand-mère ?**
   What does Mia discover in her grandmother's attic?
   a) **Une vieille voiture -** *An old car*
   b) **Une horloge -** *A clock*
   c) **Un ordinateur portable -** *A laptop*

2. **Qu'est-ce que fait Mia lorsqu'elle nettoie l'horloge ?**
   What does Mia do when she cleans the clock?
   a) **Elle la jette -** *She throws it away*
   b) **Elle la répare -** *She repairs it*
   c) **Elle tourne les aiguilles à l'envers -** *She turns the hands backwards*

3. **Qu'est-ce qu'il se passe lorsque Mia tourne les aiguilles à l'envers ?**
   What happens when Mia turns the clock hands backwards?
   a) **Rien -** *Nothing*
   b) **Elle est transportée dans le futur -** *She is transported to the future*
   c) **Elle est transportée dans le passé -** *She is transported to the past*

4. **Dans quelle époque est-ce que Mia se retrouve transportée en tournant les aiguilles de l'horloge dans l'autre sens ?**
   In which era is Mia transported when she turns the clock hands in the opposite direction?
   a) **Les années 1950 -** *The 1950s*
   b) **Les années 1920 -** *The 1920s*
   c) **Les années 2160 -** *The 2160s*

5. **Quels appareils incroyables est-ce que les gens montrent à Mia lorsqu'elle voyage dans les années 2160 ?**
   What incredible devices do people show Mia when she travels in 2160s?
   a) **Des voitures volantes et des ordinateurs portables ultra-compacts -** *Flying cars and ultra-compact laptops*
   b) **Des téléphones à cadran et des appareils photo jetables -** *Dial phones and disposable cameras*
   c) **Des magnétophones et des ordinateurs de bureau -** *Tape recorders and desktop computers*

Short Answer Questions

1. **Où est-ce qu'elle a trouvé l'horloge ?**
   Where did she find the clock?

   _____

   _____

2. **Dans quelle année est-ce que Mia se retrouve transportée la première fois ?**
   In what year does Mia find herself transported the first time?

   _____

   _____

3. **Qui est-ce qu'elle rencontre dans le passé ?**
   Who does she meet in the past?

   _____

   _____

4. **Comment est-ce que Mia retourne dans le présent ?**
   How does Mia return to the present?

   _____

   _____

5. **Est-ce que Mia veut voyager dans le temps à nouveau ?**
   Does Mia want to time travel again?

   _____

   _____

CHAPTER 24

Halloween

Aujourd'hui, c'est le trente et un octobre. C'est Halloween. **Les enfants** sont **impatients** de **mettre** leurs **déguisements** et de **recevoir des bonbons**. Marie, une petite fille de six ans, a choisi de **se déguiser** en **sorcière**. Elle a mis **une robe noire**, **un chapeau pointu** et **des bottes noires**.

Marie est prête pour sortir avec ses amis, Tom et Léo. Ensemble, avec les parents de Tom, ils marchent dans **les rues** sombres du **village**. Les maisons **sont décorées** avec des **citrouilles lumineuses** et des **fantômes effrayants**. Les enfants vont **de porte en porte** et crient «**Des bonbons ou un sort !**».

Ils reçoivent des bonbons et **des chocolats** de toutes sortes. Ils sont très contents et continuent à marcher. Ils cherchent de nouvelles **maisons** pour recevoir plus de bonbons.

Mais tout à coup, **les lumières** du village **s'éteignent**. C'est **étrange** ! Les enfants **sont terrifiés**. Tout est sombre et silencieux. Les parents de Tom leurs disent de ne pas s'inquiéter. C'est seulement **une coupure de courant**.

Finalement, les lumières **se rallument**. Les enfants continuent **leur chasse** aux bonbons en riant et en criant «Des bonbons ou un sort !».

Arrivés à la maison, ils vident **leurs sacs** à bonbons et **comptent** leurs bonbons. Ils ont assez de bonbons pour les six prochains mois. Leurs parents les laissent **manger** quelques bonbons avant de ranger **le reste** pour les prochains mois. Les enfants peuvent manger quelques bonbons chaque jour à condition qu'ils **se brossent les dents** juste après.

〰〰〰〰〰

Halloween

Today is October thirty-first. It's Halloween. The children are excited to put on their costumes and receive candy. Marie, a six-year-old girl, chose to dress up as a witch. She put on a black dress, a pointed hat, and black boots.

Marie is ready to go out with her friends, Tom and Leo. Together with Tom's parents, they walk through the dark streets of the village. The houses are decorated with glowing pumpkins and scary ghosts. The children go from door to door and shout, "Trick or treat!".

They receive candy and chocolate of all kinds. They are very happy and keep walking. They look for new houses to receive more candy.

But suddenly, the lights in the village go out. It's strange! The children are terrified. Everything is dark and silent. Tom's parents tell them not to worry. It's just a power outage.

Finally, the lights come back on. The children continue their candy hunt, laughing and shouting, "Trick or treat!".

When they arrive home, they empty their candy bags and count their candies. They have enough candy for the next six months. Their parents let them eat some candy before putting the rest away for the next few months. The children can eat some candy each day as long as they brush their teeth right after.

Vocabulary

Les enfants nm - Children

Impatient - Impatiente adj - Impatient

Mettre v - To put on

Un déguisement nm - A costume

Recevoir v - To receive

Un bonbon nm - A candy

Se déguiser v - To dress up

Une sorcière nf - A witch

Une robe noire nf - A black dress

Un chapeau pointu nm - A pointed hat

Des bottes noires nf - Black boots

Une rue nf - A street

Un village nm - A village

Être décoré(e) v - To be decorated

Une citrouille lumineuse nf - A light-up pumpkin

Un fantôme effrayant nm - A scary ghost

De porte en porte - From door to door

Des bonbons ou un sort - Trick or treat

Du chocolat nm - Chocolate

Une maison nf - A house

La lumière nf - The light

S'éteindre v - To turn off

Étrange adj - Strange

Être terrifié(e) v - To be terrified

Une coupure de courant nf - A power outage

Se rallumer v - To turn back on

Une chasse nf - A hunt

Un sac nm - A bag

Compter v - To count

Manger v - To eat

Le reste nm - The rest

Se brosser les dents - To brush their teeth

Multiple Choice Questions

1. **Quelle est la fête célébrée dans le texte ?**

   What is the celebration in the text?

   a) **La Saint-Valentin** - *Valentine's Day*

   b) **La fête des mères -** *Mother's Day*

   c) **Halloween -** *Halloween*

   d) **Pâques -** *Easter*

2. **Quel âge a Marie ?**

   How old is Marie?

   a) **Cinq ans -** *Five years old*

   b) **Six ans -** *Six years old*

   c) **Sept ans -** *Seven years old*

   d) **Huit ans -** *Eight years old*

3. **En quoi est-ce que Marie s'est déguisée ?**

   What did Marie dress up as?

   a) **En citrouille -** *Pumpkin*

   b) **En vampire -** *Vampire*

   c) **En sorcière -** *Witch*

   d) **En fantôme -** *Ghost*

4. **Avec qui est-ce que Marie va pour chercher des bonbons ?**

   Who did Marie go trick-or-treating with?

   a) **Ses parents -** *Her parents*

   b) **Ses grands-parents** - *Her grandparents*

   c) **Ses amis Tom et Léo -** *Her friends Tom and Leo*

   d) **Ses cousins -** *Her cousins*

5. **Qu'est-ce qu'il se passe quand les lumières du village s'éteignent ?**

   What happens when the village lights go out?

   a) **Les enfants reçoivent des bonbons -** *The children receive candy*

   b) **Les enfants rentrent chez eux -** *The children go home*

   c) **Les enfants continuent de chercher des bonbons -**
   The children continue to search for candy

   d) **Les enfants sont terrifiés -** *The children are terrified*

Short Answer Questions

1. **Quelle est la date aujourd'hui ?**
   What is the date today?

   _____

   _____

2. **Quel est le nom de la petite fille qui s'est déguisée en sorcière ?**
   What is the name of the little girl who dressed up as a witch?

   _____

   _____

3. **Comment est-ce que les maisons sont décorées pour Halloween ?**
   How are the houses decorated for Halloween?

   _____

   _____

4. **Qu'est-ce que les enfants disent en allant de porte en porte ?**
   What do the children say when they go from door to door?

   _____

   _____

5. **Qu'est-ce que les enfants font en arrivant à la maison ?**
   What do the children do when they arrive home?

   _____

   _____

Notes

CHAPTER 25

Où sont mes clés ?

Je suis en train de me préparer pour **sortir**. J'ai mis **mes chaussures**, **mon manteau** et j'ai **mon sac à main**. Mais il y a **un problème** : je ne **trouve** pas **mes clés**. J'ai cherché dans tous **les endroits** où elles pourraient être, mais je ne les vois **nulle part**.

Je commence à **paniquer**. Comment est-ce que je vais sortir si je ne peux pas **fermer la porte** de chez moi ? J'ai regardé dans **les poches** de mon manteau, dans **le tiroir** de la commode et sur **la table de la cuisine**. Mais **rien**.

Il existe **un double des clés** mais c'est mon copain qui les a. Cela fait plusieurs heures qu'il est au travail. J'ai essayé de l'appeler pour savoir s'il a mes clés mais il ne répond pas. Il est sûrement occupé.

Finalement, je décide de vérifier mon sac à main une dernière fois. Je mets ma main dans le sac et je sens **quelque chose** de **dur** et **froid**. Ce sont mes clés ! Je ne comprends pas comment je ne les ai pas trouvées avant. J'ai vérifié mon sac à main **trois fois** !

C'est la deuxième fois que je perds mes clés cette semaine, et on est seulement mercredi.

Je mets mon manteau et je me dépêche de sortir car je suis en retard pour aller au travail. Ce soir, je vais m'arrêter **au magasin** pour **faire un double** de mes clés. Si j'ai trois **jeux de clés**, je ne devrais pas les **perdre** aussi souvent.

~~~~~~

Where Are My Keys?

I am getting ready to leave. I put on my shoes and coat, and I have my handbag. But there's a problem: I can't find my keys. I've searched everywhere they could be, but I don't see them anywhere.

I'm starting to panic. How am I going to leave if I can't lock the door of my house? I looked in the pockets of my coat, in the dresser drawer, and on the kitchen table. But nothing.

There's a spare set of keys, but my boyfriend has them. He's been at work for several hours. I tried calling him to see if he has my keys, but he's not answering. He's probably busy.

Finally, I decide to check my handbag one last time. I put my hand in the bag and feel something hard and cold. It's my keys! I don't understand how I didn't find them before. I checked my handbag three times!

This is the second time I've lost my keys this week, and it's only Wednesday.

I put on my coat and hurry out because I'm late for work. Tonight, I'm going to stop by the store to make a duplicate of my keys. If I have three sets of keys, I shouldn't lose them as often.

Vocabulary

Sortir v - To go out

Des chaussures nf - Shoes

Un manteau nm - A coat

Un sac à main nm - A handbag

Un problème nm - A problem

Trouver v - To find

Une clé nf - A key

Un endroit nm - A place

Nulle part adv - Nowhere

Paniquer v - To panic

Fermer la porte v - To close the door

Une poche nm - A pocket

Un tiroir nm - A drawer

La table de la cuisine nf - A kitchen table

Rien pr - Nothing

Un double des clés nm - Spare keys

Quelque chose pr - Something

Dur - Dure adj - Hard

Froid - Froide adj - Cold

Trois fois - Three times

Un magasin nm - A store

Faire un double - To make a duplicate

Un jeu de clés nm - A set of keys

Perdre v - To lose

Multiple Choice Questions

1. **Qu'est-ce qu'elle ne trouve pas ?**
   What is she unable to find?
   a) **Son sac à main -** *Her purse*
   b) **Ses clés -** *Her keys*
   c) **Sa commode -** *Her dresser*

2. **Où est-ce qu'elle a cherché ?**

   Where did she looked?

   a) **Dans la salle de bain -** *In the bathroom*

   b) **Dans sa chambre -** *In the bedroom*

   c) **Dans la cuisine -** *In the kitchen*

3. **Pourquoi est-ce que son copain ne répond pas au téléphone ?**

   Why isn't her boyfriend answering the phone?

   a) **Car il est occupé au travail -** *Because he's busy at work*

   b) **Car il est au cinéma -** *Because he's at the movies*

   c) **Car il ne veut pas lui parler -** *Because he doesn't want to talk to her*

4. **Où est-ce qu'elle trouve ses clés finalement ?**

   Where does she finally find her keys?

   a) **Dans le tiroir de la commode -** *In the dresser drawer*

   b) **Dans son sac à main -** *In her purse*

   c) **Sur la table de la cuisine -** *On the kitchen table*

5. **Qu'est-ce qu'elle va faire ce soir ?**

   What is she going to do tonight?

   a) **Aller au travail -** *Go to work*

   b) **Aller faire les courses -** *Go grocery shopping*

   c) **Faire un double des clés -** *Get a spare key made*

Short Answer Questions

1. **Qu'est-ce qu'elle a perdu ?**

   What did she lose?

   _____

   _____

2. **Qui a le double des clés ?**

   Who has the spare keys?

   _____

   _____

3. **Combien de fois est-ce qu'elle a perdu ses clés cette semaine ?**

   How many times has she lost her keys this week?

   _____

   _____

4. **Est-ce qu'elle est en retard pour aller au travail ?**

   Is she late for work?

   _____

   _____

5. **Pourquoi est-ce qu'elle va au magasin ce soir ?**

   Why is she going to the store tonight?

   _____

   _____

CHAPTER 26

Les légumes

Les légumes sont bons pour **la santé** mais c'est parfois difficile à manger. J'aime certains légumes, mais pas tous. Je **préfère** les légumes classiques comme **les carottes**, **le chou-fleur**, **le brocoli** et **les haricots verts**. Je mange ces quatre légumes presque tous les jours.

J'essaye de manger d'autres légumes de temps en temps pour leur apport en **vitamines**, en **minéraux** et en **fibres**. C'est important de **varier son alimentation**. **Notre corps** a besoin de beaucoup de nutriments et les légumes sont parfaits pour ça.

Le légume que je **déteste**, c'est **la betterave**. Je l'**ai goûtée** plusieurs fois mais je ne l'aime pas du tout. **Le goût** n'est vraiment pas bon et la texture est bizarre. Même si **un plat** contient un tout petit peu de betterave, je n'arrive pas à le manger.

Une bonne façon de manger plus de légumes, c'est de les intégrer à d'autres **recettes** ou de les manger en **soupe**. Il y a beaucoup de recettes simples pour préparer les légumes. La façon la plus simple et la plus savoureuse de préparer des légumes, c'est de les **cuire** au **four** avec un peu d'**huile** et un peu de **sel**.

Je sais que c'est meilleur d'acheter des **légumes frais** mais parfois je n'ai pas le temps de les préparer. Quand je n'ai pas le temps de les **éplucher** et de les **couper**, j'utilise **des légumes surgelés** pré-coupés ou des **mélanges de légumes** pour une préparation rapide et facile. Au moins, je mange plus de légumes, même s'ils ne sont pas frais.

~~~~~~~~~~

Vegetables

Vegetables are good for your health but sometimes difficult to eat. I like some vegetables, but not all. I prefer classic vegetables like carrots, cauliflower, broccoli, and green beans. I eat these four vegetables almost every day.

I try to eat other vegetables from time to time for their vitamins, minerals, and fiber content. It's important to vary your diet. Our bodies need a lot of nutrients and vegetables are perfect for that.

The vegetable I hate is beetroot. I've tasted it several times, but I don't like it at all. The taste is really not good, and the texture is weird. Even if a dish contains a tiny bit of beet, I can't eat it.

A good way to eat more vegetables is to incorporate them into other recipes or to eat them in soup. There are many simple recipes for preparing vegetables. The easiest and most delicious way to prepare vegetables is to roast them in the oven with a little oil and salt.

I know it's better to buy fresh vegetables but sometimes I don't have time to prepare them. When I don't have time to peel and chop them, I use pre-cut frozen vegetables or vegetable blends for quick and easy preparation. At least I eat more vegetables, even if they're not fresh.

Vocabulary

La santé nf - Health

Préférer v - To prefer

Une carotte nf - A carrot

Un chou-fleur nm - A cauliflower

Un brocoli nm - A broccoli

Un haricot vert nm - A green bean

Varier son alimentation - To vary one's diet

Une vitamine nf - A vitamin

Des minéraux nm - Minerals

Des fibres nf - Fiber

Le corps nm - The body

Détester v - To hate

Une betterave nf - A beetroot

Goûter v - To taste

Le goût nm - The taste

Un plat nm - A dish

Une recette nf - A recipe

Une soupe nf - A soup

Cuire v - To cook

Un four nm - An oven

De l'huile nf - Oil

Du sel nm - Salt

Des légumes frais nm - Fresh vegetables

Éplucher v - To peel

Couper v - To cut

Des légumes surgelés nm - Frozen vegetables

Un mélange de légumes nm - A mix of vegetables

Multiple Choice Questions

1. **Quels sont ses légumes préférés ?**

   What are her favorite vegetables?

   a) **Les carottes, le chou-fleur, le brocoli et les haricots verts -**
   Carrots, cauliflower, broccoli, green beans

   b) **Les poivrons, les courgettes et les épinards -** *Bell peppers, zucchini, spinach*

   c) **Les tomates, les aubergines et les oignons -** *Tomatoes, eggplants, onions*

2. **Pourquoi est-il important de varier son alimentation en incluant des légumes différents ?**

   Why is it important to vary your diet by including different vegetables?

   a) **Pour perdre du poids -** *To lose weight*

   b) **Pour économiser de l'argent -** *To save money*

   c) **Parce qu'ils contiennent des vitamines, des minéraux et des fibres -**
   Because they contain vitamins, minerals, and fiber

3. **Quelle est sa méthode de cuisson préférée pour les légumes ?**

   What is her favorite cooking method for vegetables?

   a) **Les faire bouillir -** *Boiling them*

   b) **Les faire revenir à la poêle -** *Sautéing them*

   c) **Les cuire au four avec un peu d'huile et de sel -**
   Roasting them with a little oil and salt

4. **Quelle est sa solution quand elle n'a pas le temps de préparer des légumes frais ?**

   What is her solution when she doesn't have time to prepare fresh vegetables?

   a) **Elle achète des légumes surgelés pré-coupés -** *She buys pre-cut frozen vegetables*

   b) **Elle va manger au fast-food -** *She goes and gets fast food*

   c) **Elle ne mange pas de légumes du tout -** *She doesn't eat vegetables at all*

   d) **Elle demande à quelqu'un d'autre de préparer les légumes -**
   She asks someone else to prepare the vegetables.

5. **Pourquoi est-ce qu'elle utilise parfois des légumes surgelés pré-coupés ou des mélanges de légumes ?**

   Why does she use pre-cut frozen vegetables or vegetable mixes?

   a) **Parce que c'est moins cher -** *Because it's cheaper*

   b) **Parce qu'elle n'a pas le temps de les préparer -**
   Because she doesn't have time to prepare them

   c) **Parce que c'est plus savoureux -** *Because it's more flavorful*

Short Answer Questions

1. **Est-ce que les légumes sont bons pour la santé ?**
    Are vegetables good for your health?

    _____

    _____

2. **Quels sont les quatre légumes qu'elle préfère manger ?**
    What are the four vegetables that the person prefers to eat?

    _____

    _____

3. **Quel légume est-ce qu'elle déteste ?**
    Which vegetable does she dislike?

    _____

    _____

4. **Quelle est la façon la plus simple et la plus savoureuse de préparer des légumes ?**
    What's the easiest and tastiest way to prepare vegetables?

    _____

    _____

5. **Est-ce qu'elle mange parfois des légumes surgelés ou des mélanges de légumes ?**
    Does she ever eat frozen vegetables or mixed vegetables?

    _____

    _____

CHAPTER 27

On va au restaurant

Je **me suis préparée** pendant une heure pour **sortir dîner** avec **mon ami** Paul. On **a prévu** de nous rendre dans **un restaurant français haut de gamme** situé dans **le centre-ville**. Cela fait des mois que je veux y aller.

Lorsque je suis arrivée au restaurant, j'étais émerveillée par **la beauté** du lieu. Les murs étaient ornés de **peintures magnifiques** et **les tables étaient décorées** avec des **nappes** blanches **impeccables** et des **petites bougies**. Paul était déjà assis à notre table.

Nous avons commencé par **commander une bouteille de vin rouge** pour accompagner nos **plats**. En **entrée**, j'ai commandé **des escargots à l'ail**. Paul n'a rien pris car il voulait garder de **la place** pour le plat. Pour **le plat principal**, Paul a commandé **le coq au vin** et j'ai pris **la même chose** que lui. Le repas était **délicieux**. Pendant le dîner, on **a discuté** de tout et de rien. On a parlé de nos emplois, de nos passe-temps et de nos plans pour l'avenir.

En **dessert**, on a partagé **un moelleux au chocolat** avec **un café**.

Après le dessert, on a continué à discuter pendant qu'on finissait la bouteille de vin. Tout à coup, il n'y avait plus que nous dans le restaurant. On s'est dépêchés de **payer l'addition** pour laisser **les serveurs fermer** et rentrer chez eux.

J'ai dit **au revoir** à Paul et je me suis dirigée vers ma voiture. Je pense que je commence à avoir **des sentiments** pour Paul. Je ne sais pas si je devrais lui dire ou pas. Je vais en parler avec **ma meilleure amie** demain.

We Are Going to the Restaurant

I spent an hour getting ready to go out to dinner with my friend Paul. We planned to go to a high-end French restaurant located in the city center. I've been wanting to go there for months.

When I arrived at the restaurant, I was amazed by the beauty of the place. The walls were adorned with beautiful paintings, and the tables were decorated with impeccable white tablecloths and small candles. Paul was already sitting at our table.

We started by ordering a bottle of red wine to accompany our meals. For starters, I ordered garlic snails. Paul didn't order anything because he wanted to save room for the main course. For the main course, Paul ordered coq au vin, and I ordered the same. The meal was delicious. During dinner, we talked about everything and nothing. We talked about our jobs, hobbies, and plans for the future.

For dessert, we shared a chocolate fondant with a coffee.

After dessert, we continued to chat as we finished the bottle of wine. Suddenly, we were the only ones left in the restaurant. We hurried to pay the bill to let the servers close and go home.

I said goodbye to Paul and headed to my car. I think I am starting to have feelings for Paul. I don't know if I should tell him or not. I'm going to talk to my best friend about it tomorrow.

Vocabulary

Se préparer v - To get ready

Sortir v - To go out

Dîner v - To have dinner

Un ami - Une amie n - A friend

Prévoir v - To plan

Un restaurant français nm - A French restaurant

Haut de gamme adj - High-end

Le centre-ville nm - The city center

La beauté nf - Beauty

Une peinture magnifique nf - A beautiful painting

Une table nf - A table

Être décoré(e) v - To be decorated

Une nappe nf - A tablecloth

Impeccable adj - Impeccable

Une petite bougie nf - A small candle

Commander v - To order

Une bouteille de vin rouge nf - A bottle of red wine

Un plat nm - A dish

Une entrée nf - An appetizer

Des escargots à l'ail nm - Garlic snails

De la place nf - Room

Un plat principal nm - A main course

Du coq au vin nm - Coq au vin

La même chose nf - The same thing

Délicieux - Délicieuse adj - Delicious

Discuter v - To chat

Le dessert nm - Dessert

Un moelleux au chocolat nm - A chocolate fondant/A chocolate cake

Un café nm - A coffee

Payer v - To pay

L'addition nf - The bill

Un serveur - Une serveuse n -
A waiter/waitress

Fermer v - To close

Au revoir - Goodbye

Des sentiments nm - Feelings

Un meilleur ami - Une meilleure amie n -
A best friend

Multiple Choice Questions

1. **Combien de temps est-ce qu'elle a passé à se préparer pour sortir dîner avec Paul ?**
   How long did she spend getting ready to go out to dinner with Paul?
   a) **Une demi-heure** - *Half an hour*
   b) **Une heure** - *An hour*
   c) **Deux heures** - *Two hours*

2. **Où se trouve le restaurant où ils vont dîner ?**
   Where is the restaurant where they are going to have dinner?
   a) **En banlieue** - *In the suburbs*
   b) **Dans le centre-ville** - *Downtown*
   c) **À la campagne** - *In the countryside*

3. **Pourquoi est-ce que Paul n'a rien pris en entrée ?**
   Why didn't Paul order an appetizer?
   a) **Parce qu'il n'aime pas les escargots à l'ail** - *Because he doesn't like garlic snails*
   b) **Parce qu'il a déjà mangé** - *Because he had already eaten*
   c) **Parce qu'il voulait garder de la place pour le plat principal** -
      Because he wanted to save room for the main course

4. **Qu'est-ce qu'elle va faire le lendemain ?**
   What is she going to do the next day?
   a) **Aller au travail** - *Go to work*
   b) **Parler avec sa meilleure amie** - *Talk to her best friend*
   c) **Retourner au restaurant** - *Go back to the restaurant*

5. **Comment était le restaurant ?**
   What was the restaurant like?
   a) **Petit et sombre** - *Small and dark*
   b) **Décoré avec des peintures abstraites** - *Decorated with abstract paintings*
   c) **Haut de gamme et décoré avec des nappes blanches impeccables
      et des petites bougies** - *High-end and decorated with impeccable white
      tablecloths and small candles*

Short Answer Questions

1. **Avec qui est-ce qu'elle va dîner ?**
   Who is she going to have dinner with?

   _____

   _____

2. **Depuis combien de temps est-ce qu'elle veut aller à ce restaurant ?**
   How long has she wanted to go to this restaurant?

   _____

   _____

3. **Qu'est-ce qu'ils ont commandé pour accompagner leurs plats ?**
   What did they order to accompany their dishes?

   _____

   _____

4. **Qu'est-ce qu'elle a commandé en entrée ?**
   What did she order as a starter?

   _____

   _____

5. **Qu'est-ce qu'ils ont choisi comme plat principal ?**
   What did they choose as a main course?

   _____

   _____

Notes

CHAPTER 28

À la plage

Hier soir, mon mari m'a demandé si je voulais **passer la journée à la plage** aujourd'hui. J'ai tout de suite dit oui ! On ne travaille pas aujourd'hui et il **fait beau**. C'est une idée **parfaite** pour **se détendre** et **profiter du soleil**.

Je **me suis réveillée** tôt ce matin pour **préparer nos affaires**. Mon mari a préparé **un** bon **pique-nique** avec **des sandwichs, des fruits** et **des boissons fraîches**. Moi, j'ai pris **nos maillots de bain, nos lunettes de soleil, des serviettes, un parasol, de la crème solaire** et **un** bon **livre**.

Quand on est arrivés à la plage, **le soleil** brillait déjà très haut dans le ciel. On **a installé** notre parasol et nos serviettes à **un endroit calme** et on a commencé à se détendre. Mon mari est allé **se baigner** pendant une heure et moi, j'ai préféré rester sur ma serviette et **lire** mon livre.

Après quelques heures, on a mangé notre pique-nique puis on a fait **une sieste**. J'avais plus d'énergie après ma sieste donc j'ai accepté d'aller me baigner avec mon mari. On a joué **dans l'eau** pendant presque deux heures. Quand on est sortis de l'eau, le soleil commençait à se coucher. On a admiré **le coucher de soleil. Le ciel** était rose et orange. Après trente minutes, on a rassemblé nos affaires.

Aux alentours de sept heures du soir, on a quitté la plage, fatigués mais heureux. Nous nous sommes promis de revenir **bientôt** et de passer plus de temps à la plage, car c'était une journée parfaite pour se détendre et **passer du temps ensemble**.

At the Beach

Yesterday evening, my husband asked me if I wanted to spend the day at the beach. I immediately said yes! We're not working today, and the weather is nice. It's a perfect idea to relax and enjoy the sun.

I woke up early this morning to prepare our things. My husband prepared a nice picnic with sandwiches, fruit, and cold drinks, and I prepared our swimsuits, sunglasses, towels, a beach umbrella, sunscreen, and a good book.

When we arrived at the beach, the sun was already shining high in the sky. We set up our beach umbrella and towels in a quiet spot and started to relax. My husband went swimming for an hour, and I preferred to stay on my towel and read my book.

After a few hours, we had our picnic and then took a nap. I had more energy after my nap, so I agreed to go swimming with my husband. We played in the water for almost two hours. When we got out of the water, the sun was starting to set. We watched the sunset. The sky was pink and orange. After thirty minutes, we gathered our things.

Around seven o'clock in the evening, we left the beach, tired but happy. We promised ourselves to come back soon and spend more time at the beach, because it was a perfect day to relax and spend time together.

Vocabulary

Passer la journée - To spend the day

La plage nf - The beach

Il fait beau - It is nice/sunny

Parfait - Parfaite adj - Perfect

Se détendre v - To relax

Profiter du soleil - To enjoy the sun

Se réveiller v - To wake up

Préparer v - To prepare

Des affaires nf - Things/Stuff

Un pique-nique nm - A picnic

Un sandwich nm - A sandwich

Un fruit nm - A fruit

Une boisson fraîche nf - A cold drink

Un maillot de bain nm - A swimsuit

Des lunettes de soleil nf - Sunglasses

Une serviette nf - A towel

Un parasol nm - A beach umbrella

De la crème solaire nf - Sunscreen

Un livre nm - A book

Le soleil nm - The sun

Installer v - To set up

Un endroit calme nm - A quiet place

Se baigner v - To swim

Lire v - To read

Une sieste nf - A nap

Dans l'eau - In the water

Le coucher de soleil nm - The sunset

Le ciel nm - The sky

Bientôt adv - Soon

Passer du temps ensemble -
To spend time together

Multiple Choice Questions

1. **Qu'est-ce que son mari a fait pendant qu'elle lisait son livre ?**

   What did her husband do while she was reading her book?

   a) **Il a dormi sur sa serviette -** *He slept on his towel*

   b) **Il a joué au frisbee avec des amis -** *He played frisbee with friends*

   c) **Il est allé se baigner pendant une heure -** *He went swimming for an hour*

2. **Qu'est-ce qu'elle a fait après avoir mangé le pique-nique ?**

   What did she do after eating the picnic?

   a) **Elle a fait une sieste -** *She took a nap*

   b) **Elle a lu un livre -** *She read a book*

   c) **Elle est allée se baigner avec son mari -**
   She went swimming with her husband

3. **Combien de temps est-ce qu'ils ont joué dans l'eau ?**

   How long did they play in the water?

   a) **Pendant presque deux heures -** *For almost two hours*

   b) **Pendant une demi-heure -** *For half an hour*

   c) **Pendant une heure et demie -** *For an hour and a half*

4. **Qu'est-ce qu'ils ont admiré après être sortis de l'eau ?**

   What did they admire after getting out of the water?

   a) **Le coucher de soleil -** *The sunset*

   b) **Les étoiles -** *The stars*

   c) **La lune -** *The moon*

5. **De quelle couleur était le ciel ?**

   What color was the sky?

   a) **Bleu -** *Blue*

   b) **Rose et orange -** *Pink and orange*

   c) **Rouge et jaune -** *Red and yellow*

Short Answer Questions

1. **Qu'est-ce que son mari lui a demandé hier soir ?**
   What did her husband ask her last night?

   _____

   _____

2. **Pourquoi est-ce qu'elle s'est réveillée tôt ce matin ?**
   Why did she wake up early this morning?

   _____

   _____

3. **Qu'est-ce que son mari a préparé pour leur pique-nique à la plage ?**
   What did her husband prepare for their beach picnic?

   _____

   _____

4. **Qu'est-ce qu'elle a pris avec elle pour leur journée à la plage ?**
   What did she bring with her for their day at the beach?

   _____

   _____

5. **À quelle heure est-ce qu'ils ont quitté la plage ?**
   What time did they leave the beach?

   _____

   _____

CHAPTER 29

Les habits

Je **m'habille** tous les matins avant d'aller à l'école. Le soir, ma mère me dit toujours de **préparer mes habits** pour le lendemain. C'est plus facile pour s'habiller le matin.

Aujourd'hui, il fait un peu froid et il va peut-être pleuvoir. Je **porte un jeans**, **des baskets**, **un t-shirt** et **un pull**. Je prends **mon anorak** avec moi au cas où il pleut quand je suis à l'école.

Je dois aussi prendre **mes habits de sport** car on a cours de gym cet après-midi.

Quand je suis partie, j'ai regretté de ne pas avoir pris **mon manteau** et **un bonnet** car il y a beaucoup de vent et il fait froid.

À l'heure du cours de gym, on va tous **se changer**. Je **change de** T-shirt et j'**enfile mon short**. C'est la dernière heure de cours donc je vais rentrer à la maison avec mes habits de sport.

Avant le dîner, je vais prendre une douche. Je mets **mon peignoir** après **la douche** et je vais regarder la télévision. Avant de manger, je mets **mon pyjama** et **des chaussettes** car j'ai froid les pieds.

Ma mère me dit qu'on doit aller **faire du shopping** ce week-end car on part en vacances bientôt. On doit acheter **des sandales**, **des jupes**, quelques shorts, un **nouveau maillot de bain** et **des sous-vêtements**. Je pense que j'ai aussi besoin d'**accessoires** comme **des lunettes de soleil**, un nouveau **sac à dos** et **une montre**. On va être bien occupées ce samedi avec tous ces **achats** !

～～～～～

Clothes

I get dressed every morning before going to school. In the evening, my mother always tells me to prepare my clothes for the next day. It's easier to get dressed in the morning.

Today, it's a bit cold and it might rain. I'm wearing jeans, sneakers, a t-shirt, and a sweater. I'm taking my parka with me in case it rains while I'm at school. I also have to take my sports clothes because we have gym class this afternoon.

When I left, I regretted not taking my coat and a hat because it's very windy and cold.

During gym class, we're all going to change. I'll change my t-shirt and put on my shorts. It's the last class of the day so I'll go home in my sports clothes.

Before dinner, I'm going to take a shower. I'll put on my bathrobe after the shower and watch TV. Before eating, I'll put on my pajamas and some socks because my feet are cold.

My mother tells me we have to go shopping this weekend because we're going on vacation soon. We have to buy sandals, skirts, some shorts, a new swimsuit, and underwear. I think I also need accessories like sunglasses, a new backpack, and a watch. We're going to be busy this Saturday with all these purchases!

Vocabulary

S'habiller v - To dress

Préparer v - To prepare

Un habit nm - A piece of clothing

Porter v - To wear

Un jeans nm - A pair of jeans

Des baskets nf - Sneakers

Un t-shirt nm - T-shirt

Un pull nm - A sweater

Un anorak nm - A raincoat/A parka

Des habits de sport nm - Sportswear

Un manteau nm - A coat

Un bonnet nm - A hat

Se changer v - To get changed

Changer de v - To change (into something)

Enfiler v - To put on (clothing)

Un short nm - Shorts

Un peignoir nm - A bathrobe

Une douche nf - A shower

Un pyjama nm - Pajamas

Des chaussettes nf - Socks

Faire du shopping v - To go shopping (not for food)

Des sandales nf - Sandals

Une jupe nf - A skirt

Nouveau - Nouvelle adj - New

Un maillot de bain nm - A swimsuit

Des sous-vêtements nm - Underwear

Un accessoire nm - An accessory

Des lunettes de soleil nf - Sunglasses

Un sac à dos nm - A backpack

Une montre nf - A watch

Un achat nm - A purchase

Multiple Choice Questions

1. **Pourquoi est-ce que sa mère lui dit de préparer ses vêtements pour le lendemain soir ?**
   Why does her mother tell her to prepare her clothes for the next day in the evening?
   a) **Car c'est plus facile le matin** - *Because it's easier in the morning*
   b) **Pour dormir plus longtemps le matin** - *To sleep longer in the morning*
   c) **Pour ne pas être en retard à l'école** - *To not be late for school*
   d) **Pour ne pas oublier ses vêtements** - *To not forget her clothes*

2. **Qu'est-ce qu'elle a pris avec elle au cas où il pleut ?**
   What did she take with her in case it rains?
   a) **Un pull** - *A sweater*
   b) **Des chaussettes** - *Socks*
   c) **Un anorak** - *A raincoat*
   d) **Un bonnet** - *A hat*

3. **Quels vêtements est-ce qu'elle doit prendre pour le cours de gym ?**
   What clothes does she need to take for gym class?
   a) **Un short et un T-shirt** - *Shorts and a T-shirt*
   b) **Un pantalon et un sweatshirt** - *Pants and a sweatshirt*
   c) **Une jupe et un chemisier** - *A skirt and a blouse*
   d) **Un jean et un pull** - *Jeans and a sweater*

4. **Pourquoi est-ce qu'elle a regretté de ne pas avoir pris son manteau et un bonnet ?**
   Why did she regret not taking her coat and hat?
   a) **Parce qu'il y a beaucoup de vent et il fait froid** - *Because it's windy and cold*
   b) **Parce qu'il pleut** - *Because it's raining*
   c) **Parce qu'il fait chaud** - *Because it's hot*
   d) **Parce qu'il y a de la neige** - *Because it's snowing*

5. **Quand est-ce qu'elle prend une douche ?**
   When does she take a shower?
   a) **Avant le petit déjeuner** - *Before breakfast*
   b) **Après le dîner** - *After dinner*
   c) **Avant le déjeuner** - *Before lunch*
   d) **Avant le dîner** - *Before dinner*

Short Answer Questions

1.   **Qu'est-ce qu'elle porte aujourd'hui ?**
     What is she wearing today?

     _____

     _____

2.   **Qu'est-ce qu'elle prend avec elle au cas où il pleut ?**
     What is she taking with her in case it rains?

     _____

     _____

3.   **Qu'est-ce qu'elle met après la douche ?**
     What does she put on after taking a shower?

     _____

     _____

4.   **Pourquoi est-ce qu'elle met des chaussettes avant de manger ?**
     Why does she put on socks before eating?

     _____

     _____

5.   **Qu'est-ce qu'elles doivent acheter ce week-end ?**
     What do they need to buy this weekend?

     _____

     _____

CHAPTER 30

Un jour de pluie

Il pleut aujourd'hui. Cela fait déjà trois jours que le temps est pluvieux et cela me rend un peu **triste**. Les enfants aimeraient **jouer dehors**, mais **la pluie** et **le vent** sont trop forts. Il faut que je trouve **des activités** pour **occuper** les enfants avant qu'ils ne **cassent** tout dans la maison.

Les enfants ont besoin de **divertissements** pour rester occupés, mais il est difficile de trouver des activités qui soient à la fois **amusantes** et qui les gardent occupés pendant plus de dix minutes. Ce matin, j'ai organisé **un tournoi** de **jeux de société** et nous avons passé trois heures à jouer ensemble. **La matinée** est passée vite.

Pour **le déjeuner**, nous avons cuisiné ensemble. On a préparé **un repas simple** avec de **la soupe** et des sandwichs. Chacun a fait son propre sandwich et j'ai ajouté **des légumes** pour qu'ils soient plus sains, mais **les enfants** ont fait la plus grande partie du travail.

Après le repas, nous allons regarder **un film** pour avoir **un moment de calme**. Pour la dernière activité de la journée, je pense que nous allons faire **un atelier de bricolage**. Mes enfants adorent être créatifs, cela les aide à développer **leur imagination**. Comme Pâques est dans quelques semaines, nous allons faire **des chapeaux** avec des oreilles de lapin.

Je suis un peu fatiguée à la fin de la journée et la maison est **en désordre**, mais au moins les enfants ont passé une bonne journée. J'espère juste qu'il ne pleuvra pas demain, car j'aimerais les emmener **au parc** pendant quelques heures pour profiter de **l'air frais**.

~~~~~~

A Rainy Day

It's raining today. It's been three days of rainy weather, making me a little sad. The kids would like to play outside, but the rain and wind are too strong. I need to find activities to keep the children busy before they break everything in the house.

Kids need entertainment to stay occupied, but it's difficult to find activities that are both fun and keep them occupied for more than ten minutes. This morning, I organized a board game tournament and we spent three hours playing together. The morning went by quickly.

For lunch, we cooked together. We prepared a simple meal with soup and sandwiches. Everyone made their own sandwich, and I added vegetables to make them healthier, but the kids did most of the work.

After lunch, we'll watch a movie for a quiet hour. For the last activity of the day, I think we'll do a craft workshop. My kids love being creative, it helps develop their imagination. Since Easter is in a few weeks, we'll make hats with bunny ears.

I'm a little tired at the end of the day, and the house is messy, but at least the kids had a good day. I hope it doesn't rain tomorrow, because I'd like to take them to the park for a few hours to enjoy the fresh air.

Vocabulary

Il pleut - It's raining

Triste adj - Sad

Jouer dehors - To play outside

La pluie nf - The rain

Le vent nm - The wind

Des activités nf - Activities

Occuper v - To keep busy

Casser v - To break

Un divertissement nm - Entertainment

Amusant - Amusante adj - Fun

Un tournoi nm - A tournament

Un jeu de société nm - A board game

La matinée nf - Morning

Le déjeuner nm - Lunch

Un repas simple nm - A simple meal

La soupe nf - Soup

Un légume nm - A vegetable

Un enfant nm - A child

Un film nm - A film

Un moment de calme nm - A quiet moment

Un atelier de bricolage nm - A craft workshop

L'imagination nf - Imagination

Un chapeau nm - A hat

En désordre adj - Messy

Le parc nf - The park

L'air frais nm - Fresh air

Multiple Choice Questions

1. **Depuis combien de temps est-ce que le temps est pluvieux ?**
   For how long has the weather been rainy?
   a) **Un jour -** *One day*
   b) **Deux jours -** *Two days*
   c) **Trois jours -** *Three days*
   d) **Quatre jours -** *Four days*

2. **Qu'est-ce que les enfants ont préparé pour le déjeuner ?**
   What did the children prepare for lunch?
   a) **Des frites et des hamburgers -** *French fries and hamburgers*
   b) **De la soupe et des sandwichs -** *Soup and sandwiches*
   c) **Des pâtes et de la viande -** *Pasta and meat*
   d) **Des pizzas maison -** *Homemade pizza*

3. **Qu'est-ce qu'ils vont faire après le déjeuner ?**
   What are they going to do after lunch?
   a) **Regarder un film -** *Watch a movie*
   b) **Faire la sieste -** *Take a nap*
   c) **Aller faire les courses -** *Go grocery shopping*
   d) **Aller au parc -** *Go to the park*

4. **Quelle est la dernière activité de la journée ?**
   What is the last activity of the day?
   a) **Une promenade en vélo -** *A bike ride*
   b) **Une séance de lecture -** *A reading session*
   c) **Un atelier de bricolage -** *A craft workshop*
   d) **Une séance de jeux vidéo -** *A video game session*

5. **Qu'est-ce qu'ils vont fabriquer lors de l'atelier de bricolage ?**
   What are they going to make during the craft workshop?
   a) **Des chapeaux avec des oreilles de lapin -** *Hats with bunny ears*
   b) **Des poupées en papier -** *Paper dolls*
   c) **Des avions en papier -** *Paper planes*
   d) **Des colliers en perles -** *Beaded necklaces*

Short Answer Questions

1. **Pourquoi est-ce qu'elle est un peu triste aujourd'hui ?**
   Why is she a little sad today?

   _____

   _____

2. **Pourquoi est-ce que les enfants ne peuvent pas jouer dehors ?**
   Why can't the children play outside?

   _____

   _____

3. **Qu'est-ce qu'elle a organisé pour les enfants ce matin ?**
   What did she organize for the children this morning?

   _____

   _____

4. **Qu'est-ce que les enfants ont mangé pour le déjeuner ?**
   What did the children eat for lunch?

   _____

   _____

5. **Qu'est-ce qu'ils vont faire pour la dernière activité de la journée ?**
   What are they going to do for the last activity of the day?

   _____

   _____

ANSWER KEY

CHAPTER 1 – On va prendre un café

1. **Qu'est-ce qu'elle va faire aujourd'hui ?**
    What is she going to do today?
    a) **Prendre un café avec son amie Léa -** *Have coffee with her friend Léa*

2. **Où se situe le café dans lequel les deux amies sont allées ?**
    Where is the café where the two friends went located?
    b) **Dans la rue principale -** *On the main street*

3. **Qu'est-ce qu'elle commande au comptoir ?**
    What did she order at the counter?
    c) **Un café avec un peu de lait et un morceau de tarte aux pommes -**
        Coffee with a bit of milk and a piece of apple pie

4. **Quand est-ce qu'elles vont se revoir ?**
    When will they see each other again?
    c) **Le mois prochain -** *Next month*

5. **Qu'est-ce que Léa doit faire après ?**
    What does Léa have to do afterwards?
    a) **Léa doit aller chercher ses enfants à l'école -**
        Léa has to pick up her children from school

~~~~~~~

1. **Avec qui est-ce qu'elle va prendre un café aujourd'hui ?**
    Elle va prendre un café avec Léa.
    She is going to have a coffee with Léa.

2. **Où est-ce qu'elles se sont rencontrées pour la première fois ?**
    Elles se sont rencontrées à l'université.
    They met at university.

3. **Est-ce qu'elles habitent encore ensemble ?**
    Non, elles n'habitent plus ensemble. Elles habitent dans deux villes différentes.
    No, they no longer live together. They live in two different cities.

4. **Qu'est-ce que Léa a commandé au comptoir ?**
    Léa a commandé un expresso et un pain au chocolat.
    Léa ordered an espresso and a "pain au chocolat."

5. **Où est-ce qu'elles sont allées après ?**
    Elles sont allées au parc pour se promener.
    They went to the park to take a walk.

CHAPTER 2 – Un repas de famille

1. **Qu'est-ce que la famille aime faire ensemble ?**
    What does the family like to do together?
    c) **Dîner ensemble** - *Have dinner together*

2. **Combien de grands-parents viennent aux dîners ?**
    How many garndparents come to the dinners?
    b) **Deux** - *Two*

3. **Comment est sa mère lors des repas de famille ?**
    How is his mother at family dinners?
    b) **Elle est stressée** - *She is stressed*

4. **Qu'est-ce que fait son oncle lors des repas de famille ?**
    What does the uncle do during family dinners?
    a) **Il se plaint** - *He complains*

5. **Qu'est-ce que sa tante s'est cassée ?**
    What did her aunt break?
    d) **La jambe** - *The leg*

---

1. **Combien de personnes sont généralement présentes au dîner ?**
    Il y a en général une dizaine de personnes au dîner.
    There are usually about ten people at the dinner.

2. **Qui est stressé lors de ces dîners ?**
    Sa mère est souvent stressée lors de ces dîners.
    Her mother is often stressed during these dinners.

3. **Qu'est-ce que son père fait pendant les dîners ?**
    Son père raconte toujours les mêmes histoires.
    Her father always tells the same stories.

4. **Qu'est-ce que ses cousins font pendant le dîner ?**
    Ses cousins jouent aux jeux vidéo.
    Her cousins play video games.

5. **Qui s'est cassé la jambe il y a quelques mois ?**
    Sa tante s'est cassé la jambe il y a quelques mois.
    Her aunt broke her leg a few months ago.

CHAPTER 3 – Je n'aime pas cuisiner

1. **Est-ce qu'elle aime cuisiner ?**
    Does she like to cook?
    b) **Non, elle trouve que cuisiner est ennuyeux -** *No, she finds cooking boring*

2. **Où est-ce qu'elle préfère manger ?**
    Where does she prefer to eat?
    b) **Au restaurant -** *At restaurants*

3. **Qui est-ce qu'elle invite à cuisiner avec elle ?**
    Who does she invite to cook with her?
    a) **Des amis -** *Friends*

4. **Comment est-ce qu'elle a rendu la cuisine plus agréable pour elle ?**
    How did she make cooking more enjoyable for herself?
    d) **Toutes les réponses précédentes sont correctes -** *All of the above answers are correct*

5. **Qu'est-ce qu'elle a acheté pour rendre la cuisine plus agréable ?**
    What did she buy to make cooking more enjoyable?
    c) **Des couteaux et des casseroles -** *Knives and pots*

~~~~~~~~~~

1. **Qu'est-ce qu'elle n'aime pas faire ?**
    Elle n'aime pas cuisiner.
    She doesn't like to cook.

2. **Pourquoi est-ce qu'elle ne peut pas manger à l'extérieur tout le temps ?**
    Elle ne peut pas manger à l'extérieur tout le temps parce que c'est cher et ce n'est pas très sain.
    She can't eat out all the time because it's expensive and not very healthy.

3. **Est-ce qu'elle aime cuisiner des plats difficiles ?**
    Non, elle n'aime pas cuisiner des plats difficiles.
    No, she doesn't like to cook difficult dishes.

4. **Qu'est-ce qu'elle a acheté ?**
    Elle a acheté des couteaux et des casseroles.
    She bought knives and pots.

5. **Quand est-ce qu'elle est fière d'elle ?**
    Elle est fière d'elle quand elle arrive à préparer un plat délicieux.
    She is proud of herself when she manages to prepare a delicious dish.

CHAPTER 4 – Une journée à Paris

1. **Pourquoi est-ce qu'elle a emménagé à Paris ?**
   Why did she move to Paris?
   c) **Pour ses études -** *For her studies*

2. **Qu'est-ce qu'elle veut faire aujourd'hui ?**
   What does she want to do today?
   a) **Visiter tous les endroits touristiques -** *Visit all the tourist spots*

3. **Où est-ce qu'elle s'est rendue après avoir déjeuné ?**
   Where did she go after having lunch?
   b) **Au musée du Louvre -** *Louvre Museum*

4. **Qu'est-ce qu'elle a mangé pour dîner ?**
   What did she eat for dinner?
   b) **Une fondue au fromage avec des pommes de terre et du pain -**
   Cheese fondue with potatoes and bread

5. **Comment est-ce qu'elle décrit sa journée à Paris ?**
   How does she describe her day in Paris?
   c) **Remplie de découvertes merveilleuses -** *Filled with wonderful discoveries*

1. **Quel moyen de transport est-ce qu'elle a pris pour aller à la tour Eiffel ?**
   Elle a pris le métro pour aller à la tour Eiffel.
   She took the metro to go to the Eiffel Tower.

2. **Qu'est-ce qu'elle a commandé pour déjeuner ?**
   Elle a commandé une quiche Lorraine avec un verre de vin rouge pour déjeuner.
   She ordered a quiche Lorraine with a glass of red wine for lunch.

3. **Pourquoi est-ce qu'elle ne peut pas visiter Notre-Dame ?**
   Elle ne peut pas visiter Notre-Dame car elle est en reconstruction depuis l'incendie de 2019.
   She cannot visit Notre Dame as it has been under reconstruction since the 2019 fire.

4. **Comment est la Joconde d'après elle ?**
   La Joconde est petite d'après elle.
   The Mona Lisa is small, according to her.

5. **Comment est-ce qu'elle décrit les plats français qu'elle a mangés ?**
   Elle décrit les plats français comme lourds.
   She describes the French dishes as heavy.

CHAPTER 5 – Les amis d'enfance

1. **Qui sont les personnages principaux de l'histoire ?**
   Who are the main characters of the story?
   b) **Lucas, Jules et Emma -** *Lucas, Jules, and Emma*

2. **Comment se connaissent Lucas, Jules et Emma ?**
   How do Lucas, Jules, and Emma know each other?
   d) **Ils sont amis d'enfance -** *They are childhood friends*

3. **Qu'est-ce que Lucas propose à ses amis ?**
   What does Lucas suggest to his friends?
   b) **De partir en voyage ensemble -** *To go on a trip together*

4. **Où est-ce que les amis décident de voyager ?**
   Where do the friends decide to travel to?
   c) **En Asie -** *Asia*

5. **Combien de temps est-ce qu'ils sont restés à Tokyo ?**
   How long did they stay in Tokyo?
   a) **Une semaine -** *One week*

---

1. **Comment s'appellent les trois amis d'enfance ?**
   Lucas, Jules et Emma.
   Lucas, Jules and Emma.

2. **Est-ce qu'ils ont grandi dans le même quartier ?**
   Oui, ils ont grandi dans le même quartier.
   Yes, they grew up in the same neighborhood.

3. **Où est-ce qu'ils ont décidé d'aller en voyage ?**
   Ils ont décidé d'aller en voyage en Asie.
   They decided to go on a trip to Asia.

4. **Combien de temps est-ce qu'ils sont restés à Bali ?**
   Ils sont restés à Bali pendant une semaine.
   They stayed in Bali for one week.

5. **Combien de temps va durer leur prochain voyage ?**
   Leur prochain voyage va durer deux semaines.
   Their next trip will last two weeks.

CHAPTER 6 – Les fruits

1. **Pourquoi est-ce que les fruits sont importants pour notre corps ?**
   Why are fruits important for our body?
   c) **Parce qu'ils nous donnent des vitamines et des nutriments -**
      Because they give us vitamins and nutrients

2. **Quels fruits peuvent être mangés avec leur peau ?**
   Which fruits can be eaten with their skin?
   a) **La pomme, la poire et les raisins -** *Apple, pear, and grapes*

3. **Quel fruit peut être mangé en crème glacée dans le texte ?**
   Which fruit can be eaten as ice cream in the text?
   c) **Les fraises -** *Strawberries*

4. **Comment est-ce qu'on appelle un mélange de plusieurs fruits ensemble ?**
   What do you call a mixture of several fruits together?
   b) **Une salade de fruits -** *A fruit salad*

5. **Comment est-ce qu'on peut consommer les raisins ?**
   How can grapes be consumed?
   a) **Comme collation ou pour faire du vin -** *As a snack or to make wine*

1. **Quels sont les fruits mentionnés dans le texte ?**
   Les fruits mentionnés dans le texte sont les pommes, les bananes, les oranges, les fraises et les raisins.
   Fruits mentioned in the text are apples, bananas, oranges, strawberries, and grapes.

2. **Est-ce qu'on peut manger la peau de l'orange ?**
   Non, on ne peut pas manger la peau de l'orange.
   No, you can't eat the orange peel.

3. **Quel est le but de la peau d'un fruit ?**
   La peau d'un fruit est là pour protéger l'intérieur du fruit.
   The peel of a fruit is there to protect the inside of the fruit.

4. **Qu'est-ce qu'une salade de fruits ?**
   Une salade de fruits est un mélange de plusieurs fruits.
   A fruit salad is a mixture of several fruits.

5. **Comment est-ce qu'on peut utiliser les pommes en cuisine ?**
   Les pommes peuvent être utilisées pour faire des tartes et de la compote de pommes.
   Apples can be used to make pies and applesauce.

CHAPTER 7 – Mon frère

1. **Depuis quel âge est-ce qu'il est à l'université ?**
   Since what age has he been at the university?
   c) **Depuis ses 18 ans -** *Since he was 18 years old*

2. **Que veut-il devenir ?**
   What does he want to become?
   a) **Docteur -** *Doctor*

3. **Comment est-ce qu'il est considéré dans sa classe ?**
   How is he considered in his class?
   c) **Comme l'un des meilleurs élèves -** *As one of the best students*

4. **Où a-t-il effectué un stage l'été dernier ?**
   Where did he do an internship last summer?
   b) **Dans un hôpital de la ville -** *At a hospital in the city*

5. **Pourquoi est-ce que son frère ne rentre pas souvent à la maison ?**
   Why doesn't his brother come home often?
   c) **Parce qu'il étudie beaucoup pour réussir ses examens -**
      Because he studies a lot to pass his exams

1. **Quel est le nom de son frère ?**
   Le nom de son frère est Nelson.
   Her brother's name is Nelson.

2. **Quel âge a son frère ?**
   Son frère a dix-neuf ans.
   Her brother is years old.

3. **Quand est son anniversaire ?**
   Son anniversaire est le dix-neuf novembre.
   His birthday is on November 19th.

4. **Qu'est-ce que son frère étudie ?**
   Il étudie pour devenir docteur.
   He is studying to become a doctor.

5. **Est-ce que son frère vit près de chez elle ?**
   Non, son frère vit loin de chez elle.
   No, her brother lives away from home.

CHAPTER 8 – Le vin

1. **Quel est le vin fabriqué à partir de raisins blancs ?**
   What is the wine made from white grapes?
   c) **Le vin blanc -** *White wine*

2. **Comment est fabriqué le rosé ?**
   How is rosé wine made?
   c) **À partir de raisins rouges, mais en laissant la peau moins longtemps -**
   From red grapes, but leaving the skin on less

3. **Quel est le vin parfait pour les apéritifs et les plats de fruits de mer ?**
   What is the perfect wine for aperitifs and seafood dishes?
   c) **Le vin blanc -** *White wine*

4. **Quel est le vin souvent servi avec des salades ou des plats d'été ?**
   What wine is often served with salads or summer dishes?
   b) **Le rosé -** *Rosé wine*

5. **Qu'est-ce que les visites de vignobles et de caves à vin offrent ?**
   What do vineyard and wine cellar tours offer?
   a) **La possibilité de découvrir comment le vin est fait -**
   The possibility of discovering how wine is made

1. **Est-ce que le vin est une boisson alcoolisée ?**
   Oui, le vin est une boisson alcoolisée.
   Yes, wine is an alcoholic beverage.

2. **Quels sont les trois types de vin ?**
   Les trois types de vin sont le vin blanc, le rosé et le vin rouge.
   The three types of wine are white wine, rosé and red wine.

3. **Avec quels plats est-ce qu'on peut boire du vin rouge ?**
   On peut boire du vin rouge avec les viandes rouges et les plats riches.
   You can drink red wine with red meat and rich dishes.

4. **Qu'est-ce que l'étiquette de la bouteille de vin donne comme informations ?**
   L'étiquette de la bouteille de vin donne des informations sur le type de vin.
   The label on the wine bottle provides information about the type of wine.

5. **Combien peuvent coûter certaines bouteilles de vin ?**
   Certaines bouteilles de vin peuvent coûter plusieurs milliers d'euros.
   Some bottles of wine can cost several thousands of euros.

CHAPTER 9 – Mon téléphone est déchargé

1. **Pourquoi est-ce qu'elle utilise son téléphone en marchant dans la rue ?**
   Why is she using her phone while walking on the street?
   b)   **Pour aller à un rendez-vous** - *To go to an appointment*

2. **Qu'est-ce qu'elle doit trouver pour charger son téléphone ?**
   What does she need to find to charge her phone?
   c)   **Trouver une prise électrique -** *Find an electrical outlet*

3. **Où est-ce qu'elle peut finalement charger son téléphone ?**
   Where can she finally charge her phone?
   c)   **Dans un café -** *In a café*

4. **Qu'est-ce qu'elle fait pendant que son téléphone charge ?**
   What does she do while her phone is charging?
   a)   **Elle commande un café et lit le journal -**
        She orders coffee and reads the newspaper

5. **Qu'est-ce qu'elle décide de toujours faire dans le futur ?**
   What does she decide to always do in the future?
   b)   **De toujours charger son téléphone avant de partir -**
        To always charge her phone before leaving

1. **Où est-ce qu'elle se trouve au début du texte ?**
   Elle est dans la rue au début du texte.
   She is on the street at the beginning of the text.

2. **Pourquoi est-ce qu'elle a besoin de son téléphone plus tard ?**
   Elle a besoin de son téléphone plus tard pour appeler un taxi pour rentrer chez elle.
   She needs her phone later to call a taxi to go back home.

3. **Est-ce qu'elle a son chargeur avec elle ?**
   Oui, elle a son chargeur avec elle.
   Yes, she has her charger with her.

4. **Où est-ce qu'elle va pour charger son téléphone ?**
   Elle va dans un café pour charger son téléphone.
   She goes to a café to charge her phone.

5. **Qu'est-ce qu'elle commande au café ?**
   Elle commande un café au café.
   She orders a coffee at the café.

CHAPTER 10 – Un voyage au ski

1. **Pourquoi est-ce que la famille Dupond est partie en voyage ?**
   Why did the Dupond family go on a trip?
   d) **Pour faire du ski -** *To go skiing*

2. **Combien de temps est-ce qu'ils ont attendu leur voyage au ski ?**
   How long did they wait for their ski trip?
   b) **Quelques semaines -** *A few weeks*

3. **Que contient leur voiture pour leur voyage au ski ?**
   What is in their car for their ski trip?
   b) **Des skis, des bâtons et des chaussures de ski -** *Skis, poles, and ski boots*

4. **Qui a acheté les forfaits de remontées mécaniques pour toute la famille ?**
   Who bought the lift tickets for the whole family?
   a) **Pierre, le papa -** *Pierre, the dad*

5. **Qu'est-ce que les enfants veulent essayer pour la première fois ?**
   What do the children want to try for the first time?
   d) **Le ski -** *Skiing*

～～～～～～

1. **Qui est un bon skieur dans la famille Dupond ?**
   Pierre, le papa, est un bon skieur.
   Pierre, the dad, is a good skier.

2. **Qu'est ce qu'Annie a pris pour les soirées en famille ?**
   Annie a pris des jeux de société pour les soirées en famille.
   Annie brought board games for the family evenings.

3. **Qu'est-ce que Lucie et Nola ont demandé à leurs parents de faire ?**
   Lucie et Nola ont demandé à leurs parents de les emmener faire de la luge.
   Lucie and Nola asked their parents to take them sledding.

4. **Pendant combien de temps la famille Dupond sera en voyage au ski ?**
   La famille Dupond sera en voyage au ski pendant dix jours.
   The Dupond family will be on a ski trip for ten days.

5. **Qu'est-ce que Pierre, le père de famille, a acheté pour toute la famille ?**
   Pierre, le père de famille, a acheté des forfaits de remontées mécaniques pour toute la famille.
   Pierre, the dad, bought lift tickets for the whole family.

CHAPTER 11 – La journée de Laura

1. **Pourquoi est-ce que Laura se lève tôt le matin ?**
    Why does Laura wake up early in the morning?
    b) **Pour se préparer pour la journée** - *To get ready for the day*

2. **Comment est-ce que Laura se détend avant de se coucher ?**
    How does Laura relax before going to bed?
    a) **En regardant un film** - *By watching a movie*

3. **Qu'est-ce que Laura fait avant de dormir pour mieux dormir ?**
    What does Laura do before sleeping to sleep better?
    b) **Elle fait une liste de ce qu'elle doit faire le lendemain** -
        She makes a list of what she needs to do the next day

4. **Qu'est-ce qu'elle va manger ce soir ?**
    What is she going to eat tonight?
    a) **Une pizza** - *A pizza*

5. **Pourquoi est-ce que Laura prend le temps de se reposer et de se détendre ?**
    Why does Laura take the time to rest and relax?
    a) **Pour être en forme le lendemain** - *To be in shape the next day*

1. **Est-ce que Laura se lève tôt ou tard ?**
    Laura se lève tôt.
    Laura gets up early.

2. **Est-ce que Laura prend une douche le matin ?**
    Oui, Laura prend une douche le matin.
    Yes, Laura takes a shower in the morning.

3. **Est-ce que Laura lit un livre avant de se coucher ?**
    Oui, Laura lit un livre avant de se coucher ?
    Yes, she reads a book before going to bed?

4. **Pourquoi est-il important pour Laura de se reposer et se détendre ?**
    Il est important pour Laura de se reposer et de se détendre pour sa santé physique
    et sa santé mentale.
    Rest and relaxation are important to Laura for her physical and mental health.

5. **Où est-ce que Laura va ce soir ?**
    Ce soir, elle va à un cours de yoga avec son ami Christian et après ils vont manger
    une pizza.
    *That evening, she is going to a yoga class with her friend Christian and after that they
    are going to eat pizza.*

CHAPTER 12 – Les cours de français

1. **Pourquoi est-ce qu'elle a décidé de prendre des cours de français ?**
   Why did she decide to take French classes?
   b) **Parce qu'elle travaille dans une entreprise internationale en France et ne parle pas bien la langue -**
   Because she works in an international company in France and does not speak the language well

2. **Quand est-ce qu'elle a commencé les cours ?**
   When did she start her classes?
   a) **Ce lundi -** *This Monday*

3. **Est-ce qu'elle a bien répondu aux questions ?**
   Did she answer the questions correctly?
   b) **Elle a répondu correctement à la moitié des questions -**
   She answered half of the questions correctly

4. **Sur quoi est-ce que la professeure se concentre ?**
   What does the teacher focus on?
   c) **Les deux -** *Both*

5. **Pourquoi est-ce qu'elle veut prendre des cours de conversation ?**
   Why does she want to take conversation classes?
   a) **Parce qu'elle veut avoir plus de facilités pour les conversations -**
   Because she wants to be more comfortable in conversations

~~~~~~~~~~

1. **Dans quel pays est-ce qu'elle travaille ?**
   Elle travaille en France.
   She works in France.

2. **Quel est le nom de sa professeure ?**
   Le nom de sa professeure est madame Lydia.
   Her teacher's name is Mrs. Lydia.

3. **Qu'est-ce que sa professeure lui donne le premier jour de cours ?**
   Sa professeure lui donne un test pour évaluer son niveau de français.
   Her teacher gives her a test to evaluate her level of French.

4. **Combien d'étudiants est-ce qu'il y a dans la classe ?**
   Il y a cinq étudiants dans la classe.
   There are five students in the class.

5. **Quel type de cours est-ce qu'elle va prendre après quelques semaines ?**
   Elle va prendre des cours de conversation.
   She will take conversation classes.

CHAPTER 13 – Je suis mlade

1. **Quand est-ce qu'elle a été chez le médecin ?**
   When did she go to the doctor?
   c) **Hier -** *Yesterday*

2. **Comment est-ce qu'elle se sent depuis quelques jours ?**
   How has she been feeling for the past few days?
   a) **Faible et fatiguée -** *Weak and tired*

3. **Qui est-ce qui lui envoie des messages ?**
   Who sends her messages?
   c) **Ses amis -** *Her friends*

4. **Qu'est-ce que le médecin recommande ?**
   What does the doctor recommend?
   b) **De se reposer autant que possible -** *To rest as much as possible*

5. **Pourquoi est-ce qu'elle ne peut pas sortir de chez elle pour voir ses amis ?**
   Why can't she leave her home to see her friends?
   c) **Parce qu'elle a peur de leur donner la grippe -**
   Because she is afraid of giving them the flu

~~~~~~~~~~

1. **Depuis quand est-ce qu'elle n'a pas été malade ?**
   Elle n'a pas été malade depuis trois ans.
   She has not been sick for three years.

2. **Quels sont ses symptômes ?**
   Elle se sent faible et fatiguée. Son corps est lourd, ses mouvements sont lents et elle n'a pas d'énergie. Elle a également de la fièvre et la tête qui tourne.
   She feels weak and tired. Her body is heavy, her movements are slow, and she has no energy. She also has a fever and dizziness.

3. **Quand est-ce qu'elle est allée chez le médecin ?**
   Elle est allée chez le médecin hier.
   She went to the doctor yesterday.

4. **Que lui a prescrit le médecin ?**
   Le médecin lui a prescrit des médicaments.
   The doctor prescribed medication for her.

5. **Où est-elle maintenant ?**
   Elle est à la maison, couchée dans son canapé.
   She is at home, lying on her couch.

CHAPTER 14 – Arthur

1. **Quelles sont les deux choses préférées d'Arthur ?**

   What are Arthur's two favorite things?

   b) **Jouer au football et jouer avec son chien Tofu -**
   Playing soccer and playing with his dog Tofu

2. **Où est-ce que les parents d'Arthur ont adopté Tofu ?**

   Where did Arthur's parents adopt Tofu?

   c) **Au refuge -** *From a shelter*

3. **Où est-ce qu'Arthur joue avec Tofu ?**

   Where does Arthur play with Tofu?

   b) **Au parc près de chez lui -** *In a park near his house*

4. **Quand est-ce qu'Arthur a entraînement de football ?**

   When does Arthur have soccer practice?

   c) **Tous les mercredis et tous les samedis -** *Every Wednesday and Saturday*

5. **Quel est le rêve d'Arthur pour l'avenir ?**

   What is Arthur's dream for the future?

   d) **Devenir footballeur professionnel et gagner la Coupe du monde -**
   To become a professional soccer player and win the World Cup

1. **Quel âge a Arthur ?**

   Arthur a 10 ans.

   Arthur is 10 years old.

2. **Est-ce qu'Arthur aime l'école ?**

   Non, Arthur n'aime pas l'école.

   No, Arthur doesn't like school.

3. **Comment s'appelle le chien d'Arthur ?**

   Le chien d'Arthur s'appelle Tofu.

   Arthur's dog's name is Tofu.

4. **Combien de matchs est-ce que l'équipe d'Arthur a gagné ?**

   L'équipe d'Arthur a gagné 4 matchs.

   Arthur's team has won 4 matches.

5. **Est-ce qu'Arthur sait ce qu'il veut faire plus tard ?**

   Oui, il veut jouer au football professionnellement.

   Yes, he wants to play soccer professionally.

CHAPTER 15 – On déménage

1. **Pourquoi est-ce qu'ils déménagent ?**
   Why are they moving?
   c) **Ils ont trouvé un appartement plus grand et lumineux -**
      They found a bigger and brighter apartment

2. **Quel est l'avantage de leur nouvel appartement ?**
   What is the advantage of their new apartment?
   a) **Il a un petit jardin -** *It has a small garden*

3. **Quand est-ce qu'ils ont commencé à préparer leur déménagement ?**
   When did they start preparing for their move?
   b) **Il y a quelques semaines -** *A few weeks ago*

4. **Comment ont-ils transporté les choses lourdes ?**
   How did they transport heavy items?
   b) **Ils ont utilisé un diable -** *They used a dolly*

5. **Qu'est-ce qu'ils ont mangé le premier soir ?**
   What did they eat on the first night?
   a) **Une pizza -** *Pizza*

~~~~~~~~~~

1. **Où se trouve le nouvel appartement ?**
   Le nouvel appartement se trouve dans un quartier agréable de la ville.
   The new apartment is located in a nice neighborhood in the city.

2. **Comment est le nouvel appartement comparé au précédent ?**
   Le nouvel appartement est plus grand et plus lumineux.
   The new apartment is bigger and brighter.

3. **Comment est-ce qu'ils ont transporté les meubles ?**
   Ils ont utilisé un diable.
   They used a dolly.

4. **Quelles boîtes est-ce qu'ils ont ouvertes en premier ?**
   Ils ont ouvert les boîtes dont ils avaient besoin directement, comme leurs habits et les ustensiles de cuisine.
   They opened the boxes they needed immediately, such as their clothes and kitchen utensils.

5. **Pourquoi est-ce qu'ils ont mangé une pizza assis par terre ?**
   Parce qu'ils n'avaient pas encore de table.
   Because they didn't have a table yet.

CHAPTER 16 – Ma voiture est en panne

1. **Qu'est-ce qui est arrivé à la voiture ?**
   What happened to the car?
   a) **Elle est tombée en panne -** *It broke down*

2. **Qu'est-ce qu'il s'est passé quand la voiture a commencé à ralentir ?**
   What happened when the car started to slow down?
   b) **Elle s'est arrêtée toute seule -** *It stopped on its own*

3. **Comment est-ce qu'elle a réagi quand la voiture est tombée en panne ?**
   How did she react when the car broke down?
   b) **Elle a ouvert le capot pour vérifier le moteur -**
   She opened the hood to check the engine

4. **Pourquoi est-ce qu'elle n'a pas pu appeler quelqu'un avec son téléphone ?**
   Why couldn't she call anyone with her phone?
   c) **Parce que son téléphone n'avait plus de batterie -**
   Because her phone ran out of battery

5. **Comment est-ce qu'elle a finalement réussi à appeler un dépanneur ?**
   How did she finally manage to call a tow truck?
   a) **En allant dans une station-service -** *By going to a gas station*

1. **Où est-ce qu'elle se trouvait quand sa voiture est tombée en panne ?**
   Elle était en train de conduire sur l'autoroute quand sa voiture est tombée en panne.
   She was driving on the highway when her car broke down.

2. **Qu'est-ce qu'elle a entendu ?**
   Elle a entendu un bruit étrange venant de sa voiture.
   She heard a strange noise coming from her car.

3. **Pourquoi est-ce qu'elle est allée à la station-service ?**
   Elle est allée à la station-service pour appeler un dépanneur.
   She went to the gas station to call a tow truck.

4. **Qu'est-ce qu'elle a fait en attendant à la station-service ?**
   Elle a bu un café et elle a lu un magazine.
   She drank coffee and read a magazine.

5. **Quel était le problème de la voiture ?**
   C'était un problème de batterie.
   It was a battery problem.

CHAPTER 17 – Être en bonne santé

1. **Quelle était la nourriture préférée de Camille ?**

   What was Camille's favorite food?

   b) **Des bonbons et des frites** - *Candies and fries*

2. **Pourquoi est-ce qu'elle se sentait souvent fatiguée ?**

   Why did she often feel tired?

   c) **Parce qu'elle ne faisait pas beaucoup d'exercice** - *Because she didn't exercise much*

3. **Qui a conseillé à Camille de prendre soin de sa santé ?**

   Who advised Camille to take care of her health?

   a) **Son docteur** - *Her doctor*

4. **Que devait faire Camille pour être en bonne santé, selon son docteur ?**

   What did Camille need to do to be healthy, according to her doctor?

   c) **Faire de l'exercice régulièrement** - *Exercise regularly*

5. **Comment est-ce que Camille se sent maintenant qu'elle prend soin de sa santé ?**

   How does Camille feel now that she's taking care of her health?

   d) **Elle est heureuse et fière de prendre soin de son corps -**

   She is happy and proud to take care of her body

1. **Qui est Camille ?**

   Camille est sa voisine.

   Camille is her neighbor.

2. **Quels sont les aliments que Camille aimait manger ?**

   Camille aimait manger des bonbons et des frites.

   Camille liked to eat candy and French fries.

3. **Quels étaient les problèmes de santé de Camille ?**

   Camille se sentait souvent fatiguée et avait des douleurs dans les jambes.

   Camille often felt tired and had leg pain.

4. **Qui a conseillé à Camille de prendre soin de sa santé ?**

   Le docteur de Camille lui a conseillé de prendre soin de sa santé.

   Camille's doctor advised her to take care of her health.

5. **Quels sont les types d'exercices que Camille a commencé à faire ?**

   Camille a commencé à se promener plus souvent, faire de la danse et des exercices de musculation.

   Camille started walking more often, dancing, and doing weightlifting exercises.

CHAPTER 18 – Acheter un cadeau

1. **Qui est Marc ?**
   Who is Marc?
   a) **Son ami -** *Her friend*

2. **Pourquoi est-ce qu'elle a choisi ce cadeau pour Marc ?**
   Why did she choose this gift for Marc?
   b) **Parce qu'elle était sûre que Marc voulait ce livre -**
   Because she was sure Marc wanted this book

3. **Pourquoi est-ce que la première librairie ne peut pas vendre le livre ?**
   Why can't the first bookstore sell the book?
   c) **Parce qu'elle n'a pas ce livre en stock -** *Because it doesn't have the book in stock*

4. **Comment est-ce que Marc réagit à son cadeau ?**
   How does Marc react to his gift?
   b) **Il est content -** *He is happy*

5. **Pourquoi est-ce que Marc la remercie quelques jours plus tard ?**
   What does Marc thank her for a few days later?
   b) **Pour le café -** *For the coffee*

~~~~~~~~~

1. **Quand est l'anniversaire de Marc ?**
   Aujourd'hui.
   Today.

2. **Qu'est-ce qu'elle a offert à Marc ?**
   Elle lui a offert un livre et un bon d'achat.
   She gave him a book and a gift card.

3. **Est-ce que la première librairie avait le livre en stock ?**
   Non, la première librairie n'avait pas le livre en stock.
   No, the first bookstore did not have the book in stock.

4. **Est-ce qu'ils ont mangé un gâteau à la fête d'anniversaire ?**
   Oui, ils ont mangé un gâteau à la fête d'anniversaire.
   Yes, they ate cake at the birthday party.

5. **Qu'est-ce que Marc lui a envoyé quelques jours plus tard ?**
   Marc lui a envoyé une photo de son café accompagné de «Merci pour le café».
   Marc sent her a picture of his coffee with "Thanks for the coffee."

CHAPTER 19 – Une pizza

1. **Quels sont les ingrédients nécessaires pour faire une pizza ?**
    What are the necessary ingredients to make a pizza?
    c) **Tous les ingrédients qu'on aime -** *All the ingredients that we like*

2. **Quel est l'ingrédient principal de la sauce tomate de Sophie ?**
    What is the main ingredient in Sophie's tomato sauce?
    a) **Des tomates pelées -** *Peeled tomatoes*

3. **Comment est-ce que Sophie fait cuire sa pizza ?**
    How does Sophie cook her pizza?
    c) **Au four -** *In the oven*

4. **Quel ingrédient est-ce qu'il manque à Sophie pour sa pizza ?**
    What ingredient is missing for Sophie's pizza?
    b) **De l'oignon -** *Onion*

5. **Qu'est-ce que Sophie ajoute pour donner plus de saveur à sa pizza ?**
    What does Sophie do to add more flavor to her pizza?
    b) **Elle ajoute de l'origan -** *She adds oregano*

～～～～～～

1. **De quoi est-ce qu'on a besoin pour faire une pâte à pizza ?**
    Pour faire une pâte à pizza, il faut de la farine, de l'eau, de la levure, du sel et de l'huile d'olive.
    To make pizza dough, you need flour, water, yeast, salt and olive oil.

2. **Pourquoi est-ce que Sophie ne mange pas de pizzas surgelées ?**
    Elle ne mange pas de pizzas surgelées car elle préfère les faire maison.
    She doesn't eat frozen pizzas because she prefers to make them at home.

3. **Qu'est-ce que Sophie ajoute pour que sa pâte soit moelleuse ?**
    Elle ajoute de l'huile d'olive pour que sa pâte soit moelleuse.
    She adds olive oil to make her dough soft.

4. **Quels ingrédients est-ce que Sophie ajoute à sa pizza ?**
    Elle ajoute des tranches de mozzarella, des champignons, des poivrons, des olives et du gruyère.
    She adds slices of mozzarella, mushrooms, peppers, olives, and gruyere.

5. **Combien de temps est-ce que Sophie laisse mijoter la sauce tomate ?**
    Elle laisse mijoter la sauce tomate pendant dix minutes.
    She lets it simmer for ten minutes.

CHAPTER 20 – Une journée au parc

1. **Qu'est-ce que les parents ont préparé pour le pique-nique ?**
    What did the parents prepare for the picnic?
    b) **Des sandwichs, des fruits et des jus de fruits -** *Sandwiches, fruits, and fruit juices*

2. **Avec quoi est-ce que les enfants jouent au parc ?**
    What are the children playing with at the park?
    d) **Un cerf-volant -** *A kite*

3. **Qu'est-ce qu'ils font après le pique-nique ?**
    What do they do after the picnic?
    a) **Ils jouent au football -** *They play soccer*

4. **Qu'est-ce que les enfants peuvent faire dans l'aire de jeux ?**
    What can the children do in the playground?
    c) **Jouer sur les balançoires, les toboggans et les échelles -**
        Play on swings, slides, and ladders

5. **Qui a gagné la partie de football ?**
    Who won the soccer game?
    b) **Les enfants -** *The children*

~~~~~~~~~

1. **Qu'est-ce que les enfants veulent faire ?**
    Les enfants veulent passer leur journée au parc.
    The children want to spend their day at the park.

2. **Où est-ce qu'ils s'installent pour manger ?**
    Ils s'installent sur une couverture sous un grand arbre.
    They settle on a blanket under a big tree.

3. **Avec quoi est-ce que les enfants s'amusent après le pique-nique ?**
    Les enfants s'amusent avec leur nouveau cerf-volant.
    The children have fun with their new kite.

4. **Qu'est-ce qu'ils font après avoir joué au football ?**
    Ils vont faire une promenade dans le parc.
    They take a walk in the park.

5. **Quels animaux est-ce qu'ils ont vu au parc ?**
    Ils ont vu des canards et des tortues.
    They saw ducks and turtles.

CHAPTER 21 – Au supermarché

1. **Qu'est-ce qu'elle a acheté au rayon des fruits et légumes ?**
   What did she buy in the fruits and vegetables section?
   b) **Des fraises, des poires, des bananes, des carottes et des brocolis -**
   Strawberries, pears, bananas, carrots and broccoli

2. **Qu'est-ce qu'elle a acheté dans l'allée des pâtes ?**
   What did she buy in the pasta aisle?
   a) **Des pâtes au blé complet et de la sauce tomate -**
   Whole wheat pasta and tomato sauce

3. **Qu'est-ce qu'elle a pris pour accompagner le repas de ce soir ?**
   What did she take to accompany tonight's meal?
   b) **Une baguette fraîche -** *Fresh baguette*

4. **Pourquoi est-ce que la caissière l'a aidée à mettre ses courses dans ses sacs ?**
   Why did the cashier help her put her groceries in her bags?
   a) **Parce que la caissière était gentille -** *Because the cashier was kind*

5. **Où est-ce qu'elle a rangé ses courses en rentrant chez elle ?**
   Where did she store her groceries when she got home?
   a) **Dans le frigo et le garde-manger** - *In the fridge and pantry*

~~~~~~~~

1. **Pourquoi est-ce qu'elle devait faire les courses ?**
   Elle devait faire les courses car les placards de la cuisine étaient vides.
   She had to go grocery shopping because the kitchen cupboards were empty.

2. **Quels fruits et légumes est-ce qu'elle a achetés ?**
   Elle a acheté des fraises, des poires, des bananes, des carottes et des brocolis.
   She bought strawberries, pears, bananas, carrots, and broccoli.

3. **Qu'est-ce qu'elle a acheté dans la section des produits laitiers ?**
   Elle a acheté du lait, des yaourts et du fromage.
   She bought milk, yogurt, and cheese.

4. **Qu'est-ce qu'elle a acheté à la boulangerie ?**
   Elle a acheté une baguette fraîche pour accompagner le repas de ce soir.
   She bought a fresh baguette to accompany tonight's meal.

5. **Qu'est-ce qu'elle fait après avoir mis les courses dans le frigo et le garde-manger ?**
   Elle commence à préparer le dîner.
   She started preparing dinner.

CHAPTER 22 – Il fait trop chaud

1. **Quelle est la situation météorologique actuelle ?**
   What is the current weather situation?
   c) **Une canicule -** *A heatwave*

2. **Que fait sa famille pour se protéger de la chaleur ?**
   What does the family do to protect themselves from the heat?
   b) **Ils ferment les rideaux -** *They close the curtains*

3. **Comment est-ce que Max, le chien, réagit à la chaleur ?**
   How does Max the dog react to the heat?
   a) **Il cherche un peu de fraîcheur -** *He seeks a little bit of coolness*

4. **Où est-ce que ses amis passent la journée pour se rafraîchir ?**
   Where do her friends spend the day to cool off?
   c) **À la piscine municipale -** *At the public pool*

5. **Qu'est-ce qu'elle espère à la fin de la canicule ?**
   What does she hope for at the end of the heatwave?
   d) **De la pluie -** *Rain*

1. **Quelle est la température actuelle ?**
   Il fait presque 40 degrés.
   It's almost 40 degrees.

2. **Comment est la chaleur ?**
   La chaleur est accablante.
   The heat is overwhelming.

3. **Pourquoi est-ce qu'ils ont fermé les rideaux ?**
   Ils ont fermé les rideaux pour garder la maison fraîche.
   They closed the curtains to keep the house cool.

4. **Comment est la piscine ?**
   La piscine est bondée.
   The pool is crowded.

5. **D'après la météo, quand est-ce que la canicule va être finie ?**
   La canicule devrait être finie la semaine prochaine d'après la météo.
   The heat wave should be over next week, according to the weather forecast.

CHAPTER 23 – Un voyage dans le temps

1. **Qu'est-ce que Mia découvre dans le grenier de sa grand-mère ?**
   What does Mia discover in her grandmother's attic?
   b) **Une horloge -** *A clock*

2. **Qu'est-ce que fait Mia lorsqu'elle nettoie l'horloge ?**
   What does Mia do when she cleans the clock?
   c) **Elle tourne les aiguilles à l'envers -** *She turns the hands backwards*

3. **Qu'est-ce qu'il se passe lorsque Mia tourne les aiguilles à l'envers ?**
   What happens when Mia turns the clock hands backwards?
   c) **Elle est transportée dans le passé -** *She is transported to the past*

4. **Dans quelle époque est-ce que Mia se retrouve transportée en tournant les aiguilles de l'horloge dans l'autre sens ?**
   In which era is Mia transported when she turns the clock hands in the opposite direction?
   c) **Les années 2160 -** *The 2160s*

5. **Quels appareils incroyables est-ce que les gens montrent à Mia lorsqu'elle voyage dans les années 2160 ?**
   What incredible devices do people show Mia when she travels in 2160s?
   a) **Des voitures volantes et des ordinateurs portables ultra-compacts -**
       Flying cars and ultra-compact laptops

~~~~~~~~~

1. **Où est-ce qu'elle a trouvé l'horloge ?**
   Elle a trouvé l'horloge dans le grenier de sa grand-mère.
   She found the clock in her grandmother's attic.

2. **Dans quelle année est-ce que Mia se retrouve transportée la première fois ?**
   Mia se retrouve transportée en 1820.
   Mia finds herself transported to 1820.

3. **Qui est-ce qu'elle rencontre dans le passé ?**
   Elle rencontre une dame qui lui explique où elle se trouve.
   She meets a lady who explains where she is.

4. **Comment est-ce que Mia retourne dans le présent ?**
   Mia retourne dans le présent en tournant les aiguilles dans la bonne direction.
   Mia returns to the present by turning the clock hands in the right direction.

5. **Est-ce que Mia veut voyager dans le temps à nouveau ?**
   Peut-être que oui, car elle pense retourner dans le futur.
   Perhaps yes, because she thinks about going back to the future.

CHAPTER 24 – Halloween

1. **Quelle est la fête célébrée dans le texte ?**
   What is the celebration in the text?
   c) **Halloween -** *Halloween*

2. **Quel âge a Marie ?**
   How old is Marie?
   b) **Six ans -** *Six years old*

3. **En quoi est-ce que Marie s'est déguisée ?**
   What did Marie dress up as?
   c) **En sorcière -** *Witch*

4. **Avec qui est-ce que Marie va pour chercher des bonbons ?**
   Who did Marie go trick-or-treating with?
   c) **Ses amis Tom et Léo -** *Her friends Tom and Leo*

5. **Qu'est-ce qu'il se passe quand les lumières du village s'éteignent ?**
   What happens when the village lights go out?
   d) **Les enfants sont terrifiés -** *The children are terrified*

1. **Quelle est la date aujourd'hui ?**
   Aujourd'hui, c'est le trente et un octobre.
   Today is October 31st.

2. **Quel est le nom de la petite fille qui s'est déguisée en sorcière ?**
   La petite fille s'appelle Marie.
   The little girl's name is Marie.

3. **Comment est-ce que les maisons sont décorées pour Halloween ?**
   Les maisons sont décorées avec des citrouilles lumineuses et des fantômes effrayants.
   The houses are decorated with glowing pumpkins and scary ghosts.

4. **Qu'est-ce que les enfants disent en allant de porte en porte ?**
   Les enfants disent "Des bonbons ou un sort !".
   The children say, "Trick or treat!".

5. **Qu'est-ce que les enfants font en arrivant à la maison ?**
   Les enfants vident leurs sacs à bonbons et comptent leurs bonbons.
   The children empty their candy bags and count their candy.

CHAPTER 25 – Où sont mes clés

1. **Qu'est-ce qu'elle ne trouve pas ?**
   What is she unable to find?
   b) **Ses clés -** *Her keys*

2. **Où est-ce qu'elle a cherché ?**
   Where did she looked?
   c) **Dans la cuisine -** *In the kitchen*

3. **Pourquoi est-ce que son copain ne répond pas au téléphone ?**
   Why isn't her boyfriend answering the phone?
   a) **Car il est occupé au travail -** *Because he's busy at work*

4. **Où est-ce qu'elle trouve ses clés finalement ?**
   Where does she finally find her keys?
   b) **Dans son sac à main -** *In her purse*

5. **Qu'est-ce qu'elle va faire ce soir ?**
   What is she going to do tonight?
   c) **Faire un double des clés -** *Get a spare key made*

1. **Qu'est-ce qu'elle a perdu ?**
   Elle a perdu ses clés.
   She lost her keys.

2. **Qui a le double des clés ?**
   C'est son copain qui a le double des clés.
   Her boyfriend has the spare keys.

3. **Combien de fois est-ce qu'elle a perdu ses clés cette semaine ?**
   Elle a perdu ses clés deux fois cette semaine.
   She has lost her keys twice this week.

4. **Est-ce qu'elle est en retard pour aller au travail ?**
   Oui, elle est en retard pour aller au travail.
   Yes, she is late for work.

5. **Pourquoi est-ce qu'elle va au magasin ce soir ?**
   Elle va au magasin pour faire un double de ses clés.
   She is going to the store to make a copy of her keys.

CHAPTER 26 – Les légumes

1. **Quels sont ses légumes préférés ?**

   What are her favorite vegetables?

   a) **Les carottes, le chou-fleur, le brocoli et les haricots verts -**

      Carrots, cauliflower, broccoli, green beans

2. **Pourquoi est-il important de varier son alimentation en incluant des légumes différents ?**

   Why is it important to vary your diet by including different vegetables?

   c) **Parce qu'ils contiennent des vitamines, des minéraux et des fibres -**

      Because they contain vitamins, minerals, and fiber

3. **Quelle est sa méthode de cuisson préférée pour les légumes ?**

   What is her favorite cooking method for vegetables?

   c) **Les cuire au four avec un peu d'huile et de sel -**

      Roasting them with a little oil and salt

4. **Quelle est sa solution quand elle n'a pas le temps de préparer des légumes frais ?**

   What is her solution when she doesn't have time to prepare fresh vegetables?

   a) **Elle achète des légumes surgelés pré-coupés -**

      She buys pre-cut frozen vegetables

5. **Pourquoi est-ce qu'elle utilise parfois des légumes surgelés pré-coupés ou des mélanges de légumes ?**

   Why does she use pre-cut frozen vegetables or vegetable mixes?

   b) **Parce qu'elle n'a pas le temps de les préparer -**

      Because she doesn't have time to prepare them

1. **Est-ce que les légumes sont bons pour la santé ?**

   Oui, les légumes sont bons pour la santé.

   Yes, vegetables are good for your health.

2. **Quels sont les quatre légumes qu'elle préfère manger ?**

   Les quatre légumes qu'elle préfère manger sont les carottes, le chou-fleur, le brocoli et les haricots verts.

   The four vegetables she prefers to eat are carrots, cauliflower, broccoli, and green beans.

3. **Quel légume est-ce qu'elle déteste ?**

   Le légume qu'elle déteste est la betterave

   The vegetable she hates is beetroot.

4. **Quelle est la façon la plus simple et la plus savoureuse de préparer des légumes ?**

   La façon la plus simple et la plus savoureuse de préparer des légumes, c'est de les cuire au four avec un peu d'huile et un peu de sel.

   The easiest and tastiest way to prepare vegetables is to cook them in the oven with a little oil and a little salt.

5. **Est-ce qu'elle mange parfois des légumes surgelés ou des mélanges de légumes ?**

   Oui, elle mange parfois des légumes surgelés ou des mélanges de légumes pour une préparation rapide et facile.

   Yes, she sometimes eats frozen vegetables or mixed vegetables for quick and easy preparation.

CHAPTER 27 – On va au restaurant

1. **Combien de temps est-ce qu'elle a passé à se préparer pour sortir dîner avec Paul ?**
   How long did she spend getting ready to go out to dinner with Paul?
   b) **Une heure -** *An hour*

2. **Où se trouve le restaurant où ils vont dîner ?**
   Where is the restaurant where they are going to have dinner?
   b) **Dans le centre-ville** - *Downtown*

3. **Pourquoi est-ce que Paul n'a rien pris en entrée ?**
   Why didn't Paul order an appetizer?
   c) **Parce qu'il voulait garder de la place pour le plat principal -**
   Because he wanted to save room for the main course

4. **Qu'est-ce qu'elle va faire le lendemain ?**
   What is she going to do the next day?
   b) **Parler avec sa meilleure amie -** *Talk to her best friend*

5. **Comment était le restaurant ?**
   What was the restaurant like?
   c) **Haut de gamme et décoré avec des nappes blanches impeccables et des petites bougies -** *High-end and decorated with impeccable white tablecloths and small candles*

~~~~~~~~~

1. **Avec qui est-ce qu'elle va dîner ?**
   Elle va dîner avec son ami Paul.
   She is going to have dinner with her friend Paul.

2. **Depuis combien de temps est-ce qu'elle veut aller à ce restaurant ?**
   Elle veut aller à ce restaurant depuis des mois.
   She has wanted to go to this restaurant for months.

3. **Qu'est-ce qu'ils ont commandé pour accompagner leurs plats ?**
   Ils ont commandé une bouteille de vin rouge.
   They ordered a bottle of red wine.

4. **Qu'est-ce qu'elle a commandé en entrée ?**
   Elle a commandé des escargots à l'ail.
   She ordered garlic snails as a starter.

5. **Qu'est-ce qu'ils ont choisi comme plat principal ?**
   Paul a commandé le coq au vin et elle a pris la même chose que lui.
   Paul ordered the coq au vin and she ordered the same thing as him.

CHAPTER 28 – À la plage

1. **Qu'est-ce que son mari a fait pendant qu'elle lisait son livre ?**
   What did her husband do while she was reading her book?
   c) **Il est allé se baigner pendant une heure -** *He went swimming for an hour*

2. **QU'est-ce qu'elle a fait après avoir mangé le pique-nique ?**
   What did she do after eating the picnic?
   a) **Elle a fait une sieste -** *She took a nap*

3. **Combien de temps est-ce qu'ils ont joué dans l'eau ?**
   How long did they play in the water?
   a) **Pendant presque deux heures -** *For almost two hours*

4. **Qu'est-ce qu'ils ont admiré après être sortis de l'eau ?**
   What did they admire after getting out of the water?
   a) **Le coucher de soleil -** *The sunset*

5. **De quelle couleur était le ciel ?**
   What color was the sky?
   b) **Rose et orange -** *Pink and orange*

~~~~~~~~

1. **Qu'est-ce que son mari lui a demandé hier soir ?**
   Son mari lui a demandé si elle voulait passer la journée à la plage aujourd'hui.
   Her husband asked her if she wanted to spend the day at the beach today.

2. **Pourquoi est-ce qu'elle s'est réveillée tôt ce matin ?**
   Elle s'est réveillée tôt ce matin pour préparer leurs affaires.
   She woke up early this morning to pack their things.

3. **Qu'est-ce que son mari a préparé pour leur pique-nique à la plage ?**
   Son mari a préparé des sandwichs, des fruits et des boissons fraîches pour leur pique-nique à la plage.
   Her husband prepared sandwiches, fruit and cold drinks for their picnic at the beach.

4. **Qu'est-ce qu'elle a pris avec elle pour leur journée à la plage ?**
   Elle a pris leurs maillots de bain, leurs lunettes de soleil, des serviettes, un parasol, de la crème solaire et un bon livre pour leur journée à la plage.
   She took their bathing suits, sunglasses, towels, beach umbrella, sunscreen and a good book for their day at the beach.

5. **À quelle heure est-ce qu'ils ont quitté la plage ?**
   Ils ont quitté la plage aux alentours de sept heures du soir.
   They left the beach around seven o'clock in the evening.

CHAPTER 29 – Les habits

1. **Pourquoi est-ce que sa mère lui dit de préparer ses vêtements pour le lendemain soir ?**
    Why does her mother tell her to prepare her clothes for the next day in the evening?

    a)   **Car c'est plus facile le matin -** *Because it's easier in the morning*

2. **Qu'est-ce qu'elle a pris avec elle au cas où il pleut ?**
    What did she take with her in case it rains?

    c)   **Un anorak -** *A raincoat*

3. **Quels vêtements est-ce qu'elle doit prendre pour le cours de gym ?**
    What clothes does she need to take for gym class?

    a)   **Un short et un T-shirt** - *Shorts and a T-shirt*

4. **Pourquoi est-ce qu'elle a regretté de ne pas avoir pris son manteau et un bonnet ?**
    Why did she regret not taking her coat and hat?

    a)   **Parce qu'il y a beaucoup de vent et il fait froid -** *Because it's windy and cold*

5. **Quand est-ce qu'elle prend une douche ?**
    When does she take a shower?

    d)   **Avant le dîner -** *Before dinner*

~~~~~~~~~~

1. **Qu'est-ce qu'elle porte aujourd'hui ?**
    Elle porte un jeans, des baskets, un t-shirt et un pull.
    She is wearing jeans, sneakers, a t-shirt, and a sweater.

2. **Qu'est-ce qu'elle prend avec elle au cas où il pleut ?**
    Elle prend son anorak avec elle au cas où il pleut quand elle est à l'école.
    She is taking her raincoat with her in case it rains when she's at school.

3. **Qu'est-ce qu'elle met après la douche ?**
    Elle met son peignoir après la douche.
    She puts on her bathrobe after taking a shower.

4. **Pourquoi est-ce qu'elle met des chaussettes avant de manger ?**
    Elle met des chaussettes car elle a froid les pieds.
    She puts on socks because she has cold feet.

5. **Qu'est-ce qu'elles doivent acheter ce week-end ?**
    Elles doivent acheter des sandales, des jupes, quelques shorts, un nouveau maillot de bain et des sous-vêtements, mais aussi des lunettes de soleil, un nouveau sac à dos et une montre.
    They need to buy sandals, skirts, some shorts, a new swimsuit, underwear, sunglasses, a new backpack, and a watch.

CHAPTER 30 – Un jour de pluie

1. **Depuis combien de temps est-ce que le temps est pluvieux ?**
   For how long has the weather been rainy?
   c) **Trois jours -** *Three days*

2. **Qu'est-ce que les enfants ont préparé pour le déjeuner ?**
   What did the children prepare for lunch?
   b) **De la soupe et des sandwichs -** *Soup and sandwiches*

3. **Qu'est-ce qu'ils vont faire après le déjeuner ?**
   What are they going to do after lunch?
   a) **Regarder un film -** *Watch a movie*

4. **Quelle est la dernière activité de la journée ?**
   What is the last activity of the day?
   c) **Un atelier de bricolage -** *A craft workshop*

5. **Qu'est-ce qu'ils vont fabriquer lors de l'atelier de bricolage ?**
   What are they going to make during the craft workshop?
   a) **Des chapeaux avec des oreilles de lapin -** *Hats with bunny ears*

1. **Pourquoi est-ce qu'elle est un peu triste aujourd'hui ?**
   Elle est un peu triste aujourd'hui parce qu'il pleut depuis trois jours et les enfants ne peuvent pas jouer dehors.
   She's a little sad today because it's been raining for three days and the children can't play outside.

2. **Pourquoi est-ce que les enfants ne peuvent pas jouer dehors ?**
   Les enfants ne peuvent pas jouer dehors parce qu'il pleut et que le vent est trop fort.
   The children can't play outside because it's raining and the wind is too strong.

3. **Qu'est-ce qu'elle a organisé pour les enfants ce matin ?**
   Elle a organisé un tournoi de jeux de société pour les enfants ce matin.
   She organized a board game tournament for the children this morning.

4. **Qu'est-ce que les enfants ont mangé pour le déjeuner ?**
   Les enfants ont mangé de la soupe et des sandwichs pour le déjeuner.
   The children ate soup and sandwiches for lunch.

5. **Qu'est-ce qu'ils vont faire pour la dernière activité de la journée ?**
   Pour la dernière activité de la journée, ils vont faire un atelier de bricolage et fabriquer des chapeaux avec des oreilles de lapin.
   For the last activity of the day, they're going to do a craft workshop and make hats with bunny ears.

FRENCH-ENGLISH GLOSSARY

A

À l'envers - Backwards
À l'extérieur adv - Outside
À l'intérieur prép - Inside
Accablant - Accablante adj - Overwhelming
Un accessoire nm - An accessory
Un achat nm - A purchase
Acheter v - To buy
Une activité nf - An activity
Une activité sportive nf - A sports activity
Des activités nf - Activities
L'addition nf - The bill
Un adulte - Une adulte n - An adult
Des affaires nf - Things/Stuff
Une aiguille nf - A hand (of a clock)
De l'ail nm - Garlic
L'air nf - Air
L'air frais nm - Fresh air
Une aire de jeux nf - A playground
Ajouter v - To add
Les aliments gras nm - Fatty foods
Une allée nf - An aisle
Aller v - To go
Une ambulance nf - An ambulance
Un ami - Une amie n - A friend
Des amis d'enfance nm - Childhood friends
Amusant - Amusante adj - Fun
Un animal - Des animaux nm - Animal/Animals
Un anniversaire nm - A birthday

Un anorak nm - A raincoat/A parka
Un apéritif nm - An aperitif
Un appareil incroyable nm - An incredible device
Un appartement nm - An apartment
Un appel vidéo nm - A video call
Appeler v - To call
Apprendre v - To learn
Un arbre nm - A tree
L'argent nm - Money
Arriver en retard - To arrive late
Un art nm - Art
Un article nm - An article
Un ascenseur nm - An elevator
L'Asie nf - Asia
Un atelier de bricolage nm - A craft workshop
L'attention nf - Attention
Au revoir - Goodbye
Une autoroute nf - A highway
L'autre sens nm - The other way
Avec le temps - With time
Avec modération - In moderation
Une aventure nf - An adventure
Avoir ... ans - To be ... years old
Avoir besoin d'aide - To need help
Avoir besoin d'eau - To need water
Avoir besoin de - To need
Avoir envie de - To want to

B

Une baguette fraîche nf - A fresh baguette
Baisser v - To decrease
Une balançoire nf - A swing
Une balle nf - A ball
Un ballon de football nm - A football/soccer ball
Une banane nf - A banana
Des baskets nf - Sneakers
Des bâtons nm - Ski poles

La batterie nf - The battery
Beau - Belle adj - Beautiful
La beauté nf - Beauty
Bête adj - Silly
Une betterave nf - A beetroot
Bien connaître - To know well
Bien s'entendre - To get along well
Bien s'entendre - To get along well

Bientôt adv - Soon

Un billet d'avion nm - An airplane ticket

Une blessure nf - An injury

Boire v - To drink

Une boisson nf - A drink

Une boisson alcoolisée nf - An alcoholic beverage

Une boisson fraîche nf - A cold drink

Une boîte nf - A box

Un bon d'achat nm - A gift card

Un bon skieur nm - A good skier

Un bonbon nm - A candy

Des bonbons ou un sort - Trick or treat

Bondé(e) adj - Crowded

La bonne direction nf - The right direction

Une bonne note nf - A good grade/mark

Un bonnet nm - A hat

Des bottes noires nf - Black boots

La boulangerie nf - The bakery

Une bouteille de vin rouge nf - A bottle of red wine

Un brocoli nm - A broccoli

Un bruit étrange nm - A strange noise

Un but nm - A goal

C

Un câble nm - A cable

Un caddie nm - A shopping cart

Un cadeau nm - A gift

Un café nm - A coffee shop - A coffee

Les caisses nf - Checkout

Le caissier - La caissière n - The cashier

Un camion nm - A truck

Un canard nm - A duck

La canicule nf - Heatwave

Le capot nm - The hood

Une carotte nf - A carrot

Un carton nm - A box

Casser v - To break

Une casserole nf - A pot

La cathédrale nf - The cathedral

Une cave à vin nf - A wine cellar

Ce qu'il se passe - What happens

Célèbre adj - Famous

Le centre-ville nm - The city center

Un cerf-volant nm - A kite

Un chalet nm - A chalet

La chaleur nf - Heat

Un champignon nm - A mushroom

Changer de v - To change (into something)

Un chapeau nm - A hat

Un chapeau pointu nm - A pointed hat

Chaque jour - Every day

Charger v - To charge

Un chargeur nm - A charger

Une chasse nf - A hunt

Chauffer v - To heat up

Des chaussettes nf - Socks

Des chaussures nf - Shoes

Des chaussures à crampons nf - Cleats

Mon chemin nm - My way

Cher - Chère adj - Expensive

Chez elle - At her home

Chez eux - At their home

Un chien nm - A dog

La Chine nf - China

Du chocolat nm - Chocolate

Un choix nm - A choice

Une chose nf - A thing

Des choses nf - Things

Un chou-fleur nm - A cauliflower

Chouette adj - Cool/nice

Le ciel nm - The sky

Une citrouille lumineuse nf - A light-up pumpki

Une classe nf - A class

Une clé nf - A key

Un client nm - A client

Le coffre nm - The trunk

Une collation nf - A snack

Un - Une collègue n - A colleague

Commander v - To order

Comme d'habitude adv - As usual

Une compote nf - A compote

Un compte en banque nm - A bank account

Compter v - To count

Le comptoir nm - The counter

Un comptoir nm - A counter

Conduire v - To drive

Un conseil nm - Advice

Content - Contente adj - Happy/pleased

Un continent nm - A continent

Convaincre v - To convince

Une conversation nf - A conversation

Du coq au vin nm - Coq au vin

Le corps nm - The body

Correctement adv - Correctly

Corsé - Corsée adj - Full-bodied

Un costume ancien nm - An old suit

Le côté nm - The side

Le coucher de soleil nm - The sunset

Une couleur nf - A color

La Coupe du monde nf - The World Cup

Couper v - To cut

Une coupure de courant nf - A power outage

Courageux - Courageuse adj - Brave

Courir v - To run

Un cours nm - A class

Un cours de conversation nm - A conversation class

Un cours de français nm - A French class

Un cours de ski nm - A ski lesson

Un cours de yoga nm - A yoga class

Court - Courte adj - Short

Mes cousins nm - My cousins

Un couteau nm - A knife

Coûter v - To cost

Une couverture nf - A blanket

Couvrir v - To cover

La crème fraîche nf - Whipped cream

Une crème glacée nf - Ice cream

De la crème solaire nf - Sunscreen

La croûte nf - The crust

Cuire v - To cook

La cuisine nf - Cuisine

Cuisiner v - To cook

D

Dans l'eau - In the water

Dans le temps - In time

La danse nf - Dance

De porte en porte - From door to door

De qualité adj - High quality

De temps en temps prép - From time to time

Déballer v - To unpack

Le décalage horaire nm - Jet lag

Décharger v - To unload

La découverte nf - The discovery

Un degré nm - A degree

Un déguisement nm - A costume

Une dégustation nf - A wine tasting

Dehors adv - Outside

Le déjeuner nm - Lunch

Délicieux - Délicieuse adj - Delicious

Un déménagement nm - A move

Déménager v - To move

Un dépanneur nm - A tow truck

La dernière année -The last year

Le dessert nm - Dessert

Un dessert nm - A dessert

Une destination nf - A destination

Détester v - To hate

Devenir v - To become

Un diable nm - A trolley/A dolly

Différent - Différente adj - Different

Difficile adj - Difficult

Une difficulté nf - A difficulty

Le dîner nm - Dinner

Dîner v - To have dinner

Discuter v - To chat

Un divertissement nm - Entertainment

Une dizaine de personnes - About ten people

Docteur - Docteure n - Doctor

Un docteur nm - A doctor

Donner v - To give

Un double des clés nm - Spare keys

Une douche nf - A shower

Une douleur nf - A pain

Dur - Dure adj - Hard

E

De l'eau nf - Water
L'eau nf - Water
Une échelle nf - A ladder
L'école nf - School
Économiser v - To save
Un email nm - An email
Emballer v - To wrap
Emménager v - To move in
Un emploi à plein temps nm - A full-time job
Un emploi du temps nm - A schedule
Chargé - **Chargée** adj - Busy
En désordre adj - Messy
En fût de chêne - In oak barrels
En stock - In stock
Un endroit calme nm - A quiet place
L'énergie nf - Energy
Un enfant nm - A child
Les enfants nm - The children
Enfiler v - To put on (clothing)
Ensoleillé - **Ensoleillée** adj - Sunny
Un entraînement nm - A practice/training session
Une entrée nf - An appetizer
Une entreprise internationale nf -
An international company
Éplucher v - To peel
Une époque nf - An era
Une équipe nf - A team
Des escargots à l'ail nm - Garlic snails
Étaler v - To spread out
Un étang nm - A pond
Une étiquette nf - A label

Étrange adj - Strange
Être à l'heure - To be on time
Être coincé(e) v - To be stuck
Être comme - To be like
Être couché(e) v - To be lying down
Être de retour - To be back
Être déchargé v - To be dead
Être décoré(e) v - To be decorated
Être doré(e) v - To be golden brown
Être en bonne santé - To be in a good health
Des aliments sains nm - Healthy foods
Être en forme - To be in shape
Être fabriqué(e) v - To be made
Être fatigué(e) v - To be tired
Être fier - **fière** - To be proud
Être organisé(e) v - To be organized
Être soulagé(e) v - To be relieved
Être stressé(e) v - To be stressed
Être terrifié(e) v - To be terrified
Être transporté(e) v - To be transported
Être vieilli(e) v - To be aged
Les études nf - Studies
Un étudiant - **Une étudiante** n - A student
Étudier v - To study
Évaluer v - To evaluate
Un exemplaire nm - A copy
De l'exercice nm - Exercise
Explorer v - To explore
Les expressions nf - Expressions
Un expresso nm - An espresso

F

Facile à faire - Easy to make
La facilité nf - Ease
Faible adj - Weak
Faire chaud v - To be hot
Faire de l'exercice v - To exercise
Faire du shopping v - To go shopping (not for food)
Faire les courses - Grocery shopping
Faire maison - Homemade
Faire nos cartons - To pack our boxes

Faire un double - To make a duplicate
Une famille nf - A family
Un fantôme effrayant nm - A scary ghost
De la farine nf - Flour
Fermer la porte v - To close the door
Fermer v - To close
Une fête d'anniversaire nf - A birthday party
Des feux de détresse nm - Hazard lights
Des fibres nf - Fiber

La fièvre nf - Fever

Un film nm - A film

Une fleur nf - A flower

Une fondue au fromage nf - Cheese fondue

Un footballeur nm - A soccer player

Un forfait nm - A ski pass

Une forme nf - A shape

Un four nm - An oven

La fraîcheur nf - Coolness

Frais - Fraîche adj - Fresh

Une fraise nf - A strawberry

Francophone adj - French-speaking

Le frigo nm - The fridge

Froid - Froide adj - Cold

Du fromage nm - Some cheese

Le fromage fondu nm - Melted cheese

Du fromage râpé nm - Grated cheese

Un fruit nm - A fruit

Fruité - Fruitée adj - Fruity

Des fruits de mer nm - Seafood

Fruits et légumes - Fruits and vegetables

Des fruits et légumes nm - Fruits and vegetables

Le futur nm - The future

G

Le garde-manger nm - The pantry

Garder v - To keep

Un gâteau nm - A cake

Une gourde nf - A water bottle

Le goût nm - The taste

Goûter v - To taste

La grammaire nf - Grammar

Un grand arbre nm - A big tree

Une grand-mère nf - A grandmother

Les grandes vacances nf - Summer break

Grandir v - To grow up

Mes grands-parents nm - My grandparents

Le grenier nm - The attic

La grippe nf - Flu

Du gruyère nm - Gruyere cheese

Guérir v - To heal

H

Un habit nm - A piece of clothing

Habiter v - To live

Des habits nm - Clothes

Des habits de sport nm - Sportswear

Des habitudes alimentaires nf - Eating habits

Un haricot vert nm - A green bean

Varier son alimentation - To vary one's diet

Haut de gamme adj - High-end

L'herbe nf - Grass

Une herbe nf - A herb

Heureux - Heureuse adj - Happy

Une histoire nf - A story

Un homme nm - A man

Un hôpital nm - A hospital

Un hôtel nm - A hotel

De l'huile nf - Oil

De l'huile d'olive nf - Olive oil

I

Une idée folle nf - A crazy idea

Il est temps - It's time

Il fait beau - It is nice/sunny

Il pleut - It's raining

L'imagination nf - Imagination

Impatient - Impatiente adj - Impatient

Impeccable adj - Impeccable

Un incendie nm - A fire

Un inconnu - Une inconnue n - A stranger

Un ingrédient nm - An ingredient

Inoubliable adj - Unforgettable

Mon frère nm - My brother

Installer v - To set up

Investir v - To invest

J

jambe nf - A leg
Jaune pâle adj - Pale yellow
Un jeans nm - A pair of jeans
Jeter v - To throw away
Un jeu de clés nm - A set of keys
Un jeu de société nm - A board game
La Joconde nf - The Mona Lisa
Jouer au football - To play soccer

Jouer au football - To play soccer
Jouer dehors - To play outside
Jouer v - To play
Un journal nm - A newspaper
journée nf - A day
Un joyeux anniversaire nm - A happy birthday
Une jupe nf - A skirt
Un jus frais nm - Fresh juice

L

Laisser v - To let
Du lait nm - Some milk
La langue nf - The language
Le long de prép - Along
Léger - Légère adj - Light
Un légume nm - A vegetable
Des légumes frais nm - Fresh vegetables
Des légumes surgelés nm - Frozen vegetables
Le lendemain nm - The next day
Lent - Lente adj - Slow
De la levure nf - Yeast

Une librairie nf - A bookstore
Lire v - To read
Une liste nf - A list
Un livre nm - A book
Un locataire - Une locataire n - A tenant
Loin de adv - Far from
Louer v - To rent
Lourd - Lourde adj - Heavy
Une luge nf - A sled
La lumière nf - The light
Des lunettes de soleil nf - Sunglasses

M

Le magasin nm - The store
Un magasin nm - A store
Un magazine nm - A magazine
Magique adj - Magical
Magnifique adj - Beautiful
Un maillot nm - A jersey/shirt
Un maillot de bain nm - A swimsuit
Une maison nf - A house
Malade adj - Sick
La maman nf - Mom
Manger au restaurant - To eat at a restaurant
Manger une pizza - To eat a pizza
Manger v - To eat
Un manteau nm - A coat
Marcher v - To walk
Un match nm - A match/game
La matinée nf - Morning
La mécanique nf - Mechanics

Le médecin nm - Doctor
Un médicament nm - Medicine
Un meilleur ami - Une meilleure amie n -
A best friend
Un mélange de légumes nm - A mix of vegetables
Mélanger v - To mix
La même chose nf - The same thing
Merci - Thank you
Ma mère nf - My mother
Une merveille nf - A wonder
Une merveille du futur nf - A wonder of the future
La météo nf - Weather forecast
Le métro nm - The metro/The subway
Mettre v - To put on
Des meubles nm - Furniture
Mieux adv - Better
Mijoter v - To simmer
Des minéraux nm - Minerals

Moelleux - Moelleuse adj - Soft
Un moelleux au chocolat nm -
A chocolate fondant/A chocolate cake
Un mois de congé nm - A month of vacation time
Un moment de calme nm - A quiet moment
Monter v - To assemble
Une montre nf - A watch

Un monument nm - A monument
Un morceau nm - A piece
Motiver v - To motivate
Un moyen nm - A way
De la mozzarella nf - Mozzarella
La musculation nf - Weightlifting
Le musée du Louvre nm - The Louvre Museum

N

Une nappe nf - A tablecloth
Nature adj - Plain
Naturellement adv - Naturally
La neige nf - Snow
Nettoyer v - To clean
Un niveau nm - A level

Un nœud nm - A bow
Nouveau - Nouvelle adj - New
Des nouvelles nf - News
La nuit nf - The night
Nulle part adv - Nowhere

O

Une occasion nf - An occasion
Occuper v - To keep busy
L'odeur nf - The smell
Une œuvre d'art nf - A work of art
Offrir v - To offer
Un oignon nm - An onion
Une olive nf - An olive

On ne sait jamais - You never know
Mon oncle nm - My uncle
Une orange nf - An orange
Un ordinateur portable nm - A laptop
L'origan nm - Oregano
L'ouverture des cadeaux nf - The opening of gifts
Ouvrir v - To open

P

Du pain nm - Bread
Un pain au chocolat nm -
A "pain au chocolat" - pastry
Paniquer v - To panic
Le papa nm - Dad
Du papier cadeau nm - Gift wrap
Le paquet cadeau nm - The gift package
Un parasol nm - A beach umbrella
Le parc nm - The park
Un parc nm - A park
Les parents nm - The parents
Mes parents nm - My parents
Parfait - Parfaite adj - Perfect
Parler v - To speak
Partager v - To share
Partir en voyage v - To go on a trip

Passer des heures - To spend hours
Passer du temps ensemble -
To spend time together
Passer du temps v - To spend time
Passer la journée - To spend the day
Passionné - Passionnée adj - Passionate
La pâte nf - Dough
Une pâte à pizza nf - Pizza dough
Des pâtes nf - Some pasta
Une pâtisserie nf - A pastry
Payer mes achats - To pay for my purchases
Payer v - To pay
La peau nf - The skin
Un peignoir nm - A bathrobe
Une peinture magnifique nf - A beautiful painting
La pelure nf - The peel

Penser v - To think

Perdre v - To lose

Mon père nm - My father

Une personnalité nf - A personality

Une personne occupée nf - A busy person

Un petit déjeuner nm - A breakfast

Un petit jardin nm - A small garden

Une petite bougie nf - A small candle

Une petite note nf - A little note

Une photo nf - A photo

Un pique-nique nm - A picnic

La piscine nf - Pool

Une pizza surgelée nf - A frozen pizza

Un placard nm - A cupboard

De la place nf - Room

La plage nf - The beach

Plaire v - To please

Planifier leur voyage - To plan their trip

Une plaque à pâtisserie nf - Baking sheet

Un plat nm - A dish

Un plat à emporter nm - Takeout food

Un plat d'été nm - A summer dish

Un plat français nm - A French dish

Un plat principal nm - A main course

Un plat riche nm - A rich dish

La pluie nf - Rain

Plus grand - Bigger

Plus lumineux - Brighter

Une poche nm - A pocket

Une poire nf - A pear

Un poivron nm - A bell pepper

Une pomme nf - An apple

Des pommes de terre nf - Potatoes

Porter v - To wear

Une portion nf - A portion

Pour dîner - For dinner

Préférer v - To prefer

Prendre des notes - To take notes

Prendre soin de soi - Take care of yourself

Prendre un café - To have coffee

Préparer v - To prepare

Presser v - To squeeze

Prévoir v - To plan

Une prise disponible nf - An available outlet

Un prix nm - A price

Un problème nm - A problem

Proche adj - Close

Des produits laitiers nm - Dairy products

Un professeur - Une professeure n - A teacher

Professionnellement adv - Professionally

Profiter du soleil - To enjoy the sun

Profiter v - To enjoy

Un projet important nm - An important project

Une promenade nf - A walk

La prononciation nf - Pronunciation

Protéger v - To protect

Un pull nm - A sweater

Un pyjama nm - Pajamas

Q

Un quartier nm - A neighborhood

Un quartier agréable nm - A nice neighborhood

Quelque chose pr - Something

Quelque part adv - Somewhere

Une question nf - A question

Une quiche lorraine nf - A quiche Lorraine

Quotidien - Quotidienne adj - Daily

R

Raconter v - To tell (a story)

Un raisin nm - A grape

Les raisins blancs nm - White grapes

Des raisins rouges nm - Red grapes

Ranger v - To arrange

Rapide adj - Fast/Quick

Un rayon nm - An aisle

Une recette nf - A recipe

Une recette simple nf - A simple recipe

Recevoir v - To receive

Récupérer v - To recover

Refroidir v - To cool down

Un refuge nm - A shelter

Régulièrement adv - Regularly

Le corps nm - The body

Une remontée mécanique nf - A ski lift

Un rendez-vous nm - An appointment

Rentrer v - To return

Réparer v - To fix

Un repas nm - A meal

Un repas de famille nm - A family meal

Un repas simple nm - A simple meal

Reposer v - To rest

Reprendre son chemin - To continue on my way

Une responsabilité nf - A responsibility

Un restaurant nm - A restaurant

Un restaurant français nm - A French restaurant

Le reste nm - The rest

Rester en bonne santé - To stay healthy

Rester en contact - To stay in touch

Rester hydraté(e) v - To stay hydrated

Rester v - To stay

Une réunion nf - A meeting

Réussir ses examens - To pass exams

Riche adj - Rich

Un rideau nm - A curtain

Rien de prévu - Nothing planned

Rien pr - Nothing

Une robe noire nf - A black dress

Le rosé nm - Rosé wine

La route nf - The road

Une rue nf - A street

Une rue pavée nf - A cobblestone street

S

S'adapter v - To adapt

S'aider v - To help each other

S'allumer v - To turn on

S'éteindre v - To turn off

S'habiller v - To get dressed

S'installer v - To settle in/ To sit

Un sac nm - A bag

Un sac à dos nm - A backpack

Un sac à main nm - A handbag

Sain - Saine adj - Healthy

Une saison nf - A season

Une salade nf - A salad

Une salade de fruits nf - A fruit salad

Des sandales nf - Sandals

Un sandwich nm - A sandwich

La santé mentale nf - Mental health

La santé physique nf - Physical health

La santé nf - Health

De la sauce tomate nf - Tomato sauce

Saupoudrer v - To sprinkle

Une saveur nf - A flavor

Mettre au four v - To put in the oven

Sceptique adj - Skeptical

Se baigner v - To swim

Se brosser les dents v - To brush one's teeth

Se casser v - To break

Se changer v - To get changed

Se coucher v - To set

Se déguiser v - To dress up

Se détendre v - To relax

Se garer v - To park

Se plaindre v - To complain

Se préparer v - To get ready

Se promener v - To take a walk

Se protéger v - To protect oneself

Se rafraîchir v - To cool down

Se rallumer v - To turn back on

Se rencontrer v - To meet

Se rendre compte v - To realize

Se rendre v - To go

Se reposer v - To rest

Se retrouver v - To get together

Se réveiller v - To wake up

Se sentir mieux v - To feel better

Aller mieux v - To get better

Se sentir perdu(e) v - To feel lost

Se sentir plus à l'aise - To feel more comfortable

Se sentir v - To feel

Se servir v - To use
Se voir v - To see each other
La section nf - The section
Du sel nm - Salt
Un sentier nm - A trail
Des sentiments nm - Feelings
Un serveur - Une serveuse n - A waiter/A waitress
La serveuse nf - The waitress
Une serviette nf - A towel
Seul - Seule adj - Alone
Un short nm - Shorts
Une sieste nf - A nap
Une situation nf - A situation
Des skis nm - Skis
Un smoothie nm - A smoothie
Ma sœur nf - My sister
La soirée nf - The evening
Une soirée nf - An evening

Le soleil nm - The sun
Une sorcière nf - A witch
La sortie nf - The exit
Sortir de chez moi - To leave my house
Sortir v - To go out
Souhaiter v - To wish
La soupe nf - Soup
Une soupe nf - A soup
Des sous-vêtements nm - Underwear
Un souvenir nm - A memory
Un stage nm - An internship
La station de ski nf - The ski resort
Une station-service nf - A gas station
Sucré - Sucrée adj - Sweet
Un supermarché nm - A supermarket
Supportable adj - Bearable
Le système immunitaire nm - Immune system

T

Un t-shirt nm - T-shirt
Une table nf - A table
La table de la cuisine nf - A kitchen table
Une tâche nf - A task
Ma tante nf - My aunt
Tard adv - Late
Une tarte nf - A pie
Une tarte aux pommes nf - Apple pie
Un taxi nm - A taxi
Un téléphone nm - A phone
La température nf - Temperature
Le terrain nm - The field
Une terrasse nf - A terrace
Un test nm - A test
La tête qui tourne nf -
Dizziness (The head spinning)
La Thaïlande nf - Thailand
Un ticket de caisse nm - A receipt
Un tiroir nm - A drawer
Un toboggan nm - A slide
Une tomate pelée nf - Peeled tomato

Tomber en panne v - To break down
Une tortue nf - A turtle
La tour Eiffel nf - The Eiffel Tower
Touristique adj - Touristic
Tourner v - To turn
Un tournoi nm - A tournament
Tous ensemble - All together
Tous les deux mois - Every two months
Tout le temps adv - All the time
Tout près adv - Very close
Une tradition nf - A tradition
Un trajet nm - A journey
Une tranche nf - A slice
Le travail nm - Work
Trébucher v - To stumble
Trier v - To sort
Triste adj - Sad
Trois fois - Three times
Trop adv - Too much
Trouver v - To find

U

Un peu de lait - A little bit of milk
Une fois par mois - Once a month
L'université nf - The university

Un ustensile nm - A utensil
Des ustensiles de cuisine nm - Kitchen utensils
Utiliser v - To use

V

Les vacances de Noël nf - Christmas holidays
Une valise nf - A suitcase
Une variété de nf - A variety of
Le vent nm - The wind
Un ventilateur nm - A fan
Un verre de vin rouge nm - A glass of red wine
Des vêtements chauds nm - Warm clothing
De la viande nf - Meat
Une viande rouge nf - Red meat
Vide adj - Empty
Une vidéo nf - A video
La vie nf - Life
Une vie nf - A life
Une vieille horloge nf - An old clock
Un vieux magasin nm - An old store
Un vignoble nm - A vineyard
Un village nm - A village

Le ville nf - The city
Du vin nm - Wine
Le vin nm - Wine
Le vin blanc nm - White wine
Le vin rouge nm - Red wine
Une visite nf - A visit
Visiter v - To visit
Une vitamine nf - A vitamin
Le vocabulaire nm - Vocabulary
Un voisin - Une voisine n - A neighbor
Une voiture nf - A car
Une voiture à chevaux nf - A horse-drawn carriage
Une voiture volante nf - A flying car
Un voyage nm - A trip
Voyager v - To travel
La vue nf - The view

W

Un week-end nm - A weekend

Y

Des yaourts nm - Some yogurts

THANK YOU

Thank you for choosing "**French Short Stories**" as your language learning companion. I sincerely hope that these stories have helped you improve your French skills and that you have enjoyed exploring the world of French literature.

As I mentioned earlier, my aim was to create a resource that would fit into even the busiest of schedules while still providing a comprehensive learning experience. I would greatly appreciate your feedback, so **please consider leaving a review on Amazon** to let me know your thoughts.

As a writer of numerous French textbooks, "**French Short Stories**" is my first storybook. I am excited to continue providing learners with engaging and effective language learning resources, and I have more French language books in the work. Stay tuned for updates!

For more free lessons, books, and workshops, please visit my website. www.theperfectfrench.com

I hope you find it helpful in your language learning journey.

Once again, thank you for choosing "**French Short Stories**." I wish you all the best in your progress in learning the beautiful French language!

Dylane